Time Capsules

By Nancy L. Johnson

Cover and Illustrations by Greg Lawhun
Graphic Production by Pam Jensen

Time Capsules is published jointly by **Pieces of Learning** and **Gary Grimm & Associates**. It is part of a grouping of products trademarked as ***Turning 2000™: Products for the New Millennium***. If you would like information about other products available please write either company.

Pieces of Learning
PO Box 340667
Dayton OH 45434-0667
1-800-729-5137
FAX 937-427-3380
www.piecesoflearning.com

Gary Grimm & Associates
82 S. Madison Street
PO Box 378
Carthage IL 62321-0378
1-800-442-1614
FAX 217-357-6763

Time Capsules by Nancy L. Johnson
© Pieces of Learning 1998
ISBN 1-880505-26-6
Printing number 9876543
All rights reserved. Printed in the United States of America.
The purchase of this book entitles the buyer to reproduce pages for his/her classroom use only. Any other use requires written permission from Pieces of Learning at 1-800-729-5137. Some images used herein were obtained from IMSI's MasterClips/MasterPhotos© Collection, 1895 Francisco Blvd. East, San Rafael, CA 94901-5506, USA.

"Children are the living messages

we send

to a time we will not see."

author unknown

Table of Contents

Introduction 4

Learner Outcomes 5

Time Capsules Are . . . Can be 6

A Time Capsule Explorer's Log 10

Constructing a Time Capsule 12

Understanding Time 15

Mini Time Capsule·
One Day 16
Five Days 19
Thirty Days 20
One School Year 21

A 10 Year Personal Time Capsule 22
My Autobiography 24
A Letter to the Future 29

A Summer Vacation Time Capsule 31

A Living Time Capsule 38

Capsules and More Capsules 41

Activities and More Activities 46

The very best time capsule ever 47

Introduction

Congratulations to us! We're making it! A new century.
A new millennium.
Our calendars are turning 2000.
It's a new time, a unique time.
It's a once-in-a-lifetime event for all of us.

The questions are . . .

....Is it time to reflect on the past and dream about the future?
....Are the past, present and future related?
....Is time a concept worthy of exploration and enjoyment?
....Is it possible for young learners to really understand what a millennium is?
....Can we really change the future?
....Can we empower learners to feel **hopeful** instead of hopeless about the future?

The answers are . . .

....Yes!....YES!....Yes!....YES!....Yes!....YES!

Time capsules are wonderful teaching and learning tools. They are visual, concrete and comprehensive. They are symbols of change. As a project or activity they offer flexibility, from independent study and cooperative learning to large group instruction.

They are thematic, combining language arts, math, social studies, science, music and art. They teach learners how to draw conclusions from implicit information. They teach learners about change; how to identify it and how to make it happen. Most of all, in this age of instant gratification, time capsules awaken the joys of anticipation, mystery and surprise for learners of all ages.

Something's Missing . . .

The word student will not be found in the activities described in this book. The word learner is used instead. The word student is connected to school, a 13 to 17 year process that ends with a diploma. In the new millennium learning must be a lifelong process. Educators, both teachers and parents, must change the old terminology of the 20th century. The new paradigm for the 21st century must include the words lifelong learning. Words are important. They make a difference. They facilitate change. Children can be more than students.

They can be LEARNERS!

Learner Outcomes

- ❑ The learner will develop the ability to find, analyze, use and present information about time capsules.

- ❑ The learner will develop the ability to communicate effectively with future generations through time capsules.

- ❑ The learner will develop the ability to form meaningful and working relationships with their peers while completing a time capsule.

- ❑ The learner will generate ideas and questions related to the broad-based issues concerning past, present and future.

- ❑ The learner will generate original ideas and questions in creating a time capsule that is unique.

- ❑ The learner will use a variety of media and artistic materials to complete a time capsule while working in a cooperative group.

- ❑ The learner will effectively interpret historical data in collecting and organizing the contents of a time capsule.

- ❑ The learner will explore the concept of time as it applies to the year 2000 and beyond.

- ❑ The learner will make comparisons between cultures, show relationships or associations between different times in history.

- ❑ The learner will develop a strong, positive attitude about the future and his/her place in it.

- ❑ The learner will demonstrate an ability to do active research in order to gather data for the completion of a time capsule.

- ❑ The gifted learner will be involved in an in-depth learning experience related to a self-directed topic involving time capsules.

- ❑ The learner will have the opportunity to appreciate the skills, abilities and learning styles of others by sharing a final product.

Time Capsules are . . .

....**memories.**

....messages from the present to the future.

....mini museums filled with souvenirs and keepsakes.

....**collections of history for history.**

....evidence.

....pieces of learning about people, places and things.

....**ideas, information and data for future generations.**

....pictures, photos, drawings, illustrations and cartoons.

....notes, poems, letters, clippings, comments and quotes.

....**hopes, promises, resolutions.**

....endings and beginnings.

....moments in time.

....**memorabilia.**

....examples.

....tributes to heroes and eulogies.

....**feelings, opinions, testimonies and points of view.**

....proof and documentation of the present.

....accumulations of honesty.
....recollections from those who are wise.
....funny, surprising and mysterious.
....a remembrance of today to be opened tomorrow.

Time Capsules can be . . .

. . . a box
    . . . a potato chip can
        . . . a plastic bag
. . . a book
    . . . an old-world forest
        . . . a sunken ship
. . . a library
    . . . an archeological dig
        . . . a photo album

. . . a coffee can
    . . . a plastic bottle
        . . . an envelope
            . . . a scrapbook
    . . . a cemetery
        . . . an attic
    . . . a person
        . . . a basement
            . . . a closet

. . . a junk yard
    . . . a tape recorder
        . . . a landfill
            . . . a museum
        . . . a file cabinet
            . . . a baby book
                . . . a cave
                    . . . an antique store
                    . . . a letter
                      . . . an art gallery

    . . . a courthouse
        . . . a great-grandma's button box
  . . . a computer disk or CD ROM
            . . . a senior citizen's mind
                . . . a cocoon
. . . great-grandpa's tool box
    . . . a last will and testament
        . . . a pair of old shoes

Time Capsules can last . . .

. . . a day   . . . a week   . . . a month

. . . a year   . . . a lifetime   . . . several lifetimes

                      . . . forever

Discussion Questions

Choose 3 Time Capsules:
    A. _____ B. _____ C. _____

1. How and why can each of the items above be considered a time capsule?
   A.
   B.
   C.
2. What span of years does each capsule cover? A. _____ B. _____ C. _____
3. What are objects and ideas that might be found in one of the capsules?

4. What would happen if one of the time capsules could talk? What would it say?

5. Who might be interested in examining one of them? Why?

6. Can you predict what "stuff" might be added to each capsule in the next ten years?
   A.
   B.
   C.

Answer the following questions on a separate sheet of paper.

> How are time capsules like bridges - connecting the past to the present?
> Which capsules would make an appropriate gift? For whom? Why?
> How can time capsules help people?
> How do time capsules "tell time"?
> How are two of the capsules alike? How are they different?
> Can time capsules predict the future? Explain.
> What if you were an official Time Capsule Judge? What rules would you follow in judging a prize-winning capsule?
> What are all the ways time capsules can be protected and saved?

Active Questioning

Compose a list of questions about each capsule. Just questions! No answers!

What if .... ?
How come .... ?
How many .... ?
Where would .... ?
Who will .... ?
When did .... ?

Activities

1. Tell a story or write a newspaper report about finding one of the capsules.

2. Go find or go visit one of the special time capsules. Do an interview. Film a video.

3. Use your active questioning list and interview one of the living capsules.

4. Create a board game that has various time capsule clues hidden under the spaces.

5. Call or write a mayor convincing him/her to bury a real time capsule under city hall.

6. Invite one of the living time capsules to come to your classroom for an interview.

7. Form a Time Capsule Club. Invite all your friends to join.

8. Organize a Time Capsule Fair, displaying many different examples of capsules.

9. Create your own unique time capsule. Ask a friend to help you.

10. Choose one of the special capsules and complete the Explorer's Log.

A Time Capsule EXPLORER'S LOG

Date capsule was discovered: Date capsule was started:

Location:

Description and condition of capsule:

Drawing/illustration/photo of capsule:

List of contents:

Drawing of three objects from capsule:

Questions and comments about the contents:

1. Why...

2. I wonder...

3. How come...

4. What if...

5. Who...

6. Is it possible that...

7. It seems like...   Describe an unsolved mystery about the capsule:

8. Maybe...   Describe a lesson for the future learned from the capsule:

Describe a history lesson learned from the capsule:

Describe a surprising discovery from the capsule:

Constructing a Time Capsule

The Basic Format

Most time capsules contain three types of information: (1) **"Now Stuff,"** (2) **Goals and Objectives** for the future, and (3) **Predictions**. Depending on the size of the container, time capsules also include objects and other memorabilia which symbolize current events, opinions and attitudes related to a specific time or era. Some time capsules are active. They are meant to be either added to slowly over a long period of time (a Baby Book Time Capsule) or completed immediately, opened and used (a Summer Vacation Time Capsule).

"Now Stuff"

This portion of a time capsule includes facts, personal observations, reflections and various other forms of data. When combined with symbols and memorabilia, it forms a body of physical evidence reflecting a specific time.

Goals and Objectives

An important component of a time capsule deals with the change process. Presented as resolutions, promises or wishes, these statements are focused on the future. They empower learners to make positive changes in their behavior and attitudes about the future.

Predictions

What fun! From guessing the outcome of future sporting events to forecasting the winner of an election, predictions can be based on sophisticated research or gut-level feelings. They form the foundation for delightful compare/contrast lessons when the time capsule is finally opened.

Memorabilia and Symbols

Time capsules can be very simple - a few pieces of paper filled with information. However, when objects, artifacts, memorabilia and other symbolic material are added the capsule "comes alive." Children with learning styles ranging from verbal to kinesthetic, visual to intuitive, can apply their skills in developing a truly unique product.

The Basic Lesson Plan

To the Teacher/Facilitator

Choose the type of time capsule to be studied and assembled. There are examples throughout this book.

Gather supplies, materials and information appropriate for that particular type of capsule.

Teaching the lesson

Pretest

Lead a discussion about capsules. (See page 8.) Compare/contrast different types of capsules; everything from medication gel capsules and seed pod capsules to space capsules, using models and pictures. Join learners in brainstorming a list of different types of capsules. Lead the discussion toward a special type of capsule - a time capsule.

Readiness

Lead a discussion about time using a clock, watch, hour glass, and sun dial. Define time capsules with examples. Share a real time capsule. (Teacher may bury a capsule on the school grounds or "bury" a time capsule someplace in the classroom.)

Spelling

Introduce the vocabulary (page 14) related to the type of time capsule being studied. Apply the vocabulary in practice sentences and creative writing. Make a mini spelling capsule by writing each word on a separate slip of paper. Put slips in a small plastic bag. Learners pick a word from the bag and use it in a sentence.

Research

Learners read, interview, survey, view videos and films, listen to music and generally gather a variety of information related to the specific theme of a capsule. The research should always be active as well as passive.

Select/Design/Decorate Container

The type of container depends on how long the capsule is to be stored and the creativity of the learner. Just remember, the longer the capsule remains unopened, the more durable the container must be. See page 7.

Gather Contents

This can take a few minutes or a few weeks. The contents include everything from pieces of paper to science experiments. The size of the contents depends on the size of the container. And remember once again, the longer the capsule is sealed, the more durable the contents need to be. For capsules of 10 or more years, sealing the contents by lamination or shrink-wrap is a great idea.

Share Completed Capsules

Comparing and contrasting capsules, before and after they are sealed, is an important part of the learning process. New ideas for future capsules always emerge from the sharing process.

Secure Capsules

Time capsules are really only valuable if they can be found at some future date, so taping them shut with duct tape, labeling and storing them in a safe place is most important. The "Keeper of the Capsule" must be a trusted, responsible person.

Vocabulary

box	bottle	calendar	capsule	carton
clock	collection	confirmation	container	data
document	documentation	estimate	future	goals
history	keepsake	memorabilia	holder	jar
memory	past	plan	prediction	present
promise	recollection	receptacle	resolutions	remembrance
sample	souvenir	span	time	cocoon
anticipation	surprise	survey	interview	

Understanding TIME: Step by Step

Philosophers have been trying to understand and explain the concept of time for generations. Only a few would claim real success. So it shouldn't be a surprise when children have the same trouble. "Is it time yet?", "How much time is left?", "Are we there yet?" and "How long until we get there?" are all too familiar statements from impatient young children who have difficulty comprehending the passage of time.

The following series of lessons will guide young learners through several fun and creative activities that will improve their understanding and attitude about time. The lessons are progressive, starting with three Mini Time Capsules that cover short periods of time culminating with a final capsule that covers an entire school year. By lengthening the time of each capsule from one day, to one week, to one month, then one year, learners begin to get a better "feel" for the passage of time. All three capsules are group capsules, with all learners contributing to one large shared capsule.

There are empty spaces and blank spots throughout the lessons for teacher/facilitator and other learners to add ideas. A review of the Basic Lesson Plan Format, Vocabulary and Learner Outcomes will also be helpful.

Note: In this age of instant gratification, the anticipation and delay in opening a time capsule is truly an important lesson for young learners.

Mini Time Capsule #1 (One Day)

Step One: Early in the year, start a school day by showing the class a small empty box labeled **Mini Time Capsule**. Explain that this time capsule is special. It only lasts one day. Learners fill the capsule in the morning and open it at the end of the school day. They collect three types of data to put in their capsule:

(1) "Now stuff," including several lists or observations about what is happening that morning
(2) Behavioral and academic goals to be accomplished by the end of the day
(3) Predictions or guesses about things that might happen by the end of the day

Near the end of the school day, open and examine the **Mini Time Capsule**. Compare/contrast the end of the day with the beginning by discussing how many "changes" occurred, which goals were achieved, and how many predictions came true.

Contents of the Mini Time Capsule:

"NOW STUFF"

- a small card or piece of paper listing date, name of school, classroom name or number, and teacher's name
- an instant photo or drawing of a clock showing the current time
- a list of learners in attendance and/or an instant photo of the entire class
- several instant photos of the classroom taken from different angles
- names/photos of those celebrating a birthday or other special event
- a brief health report about those in attendance
- a schedule of planned activities for the day
- a brief written weather report along with an instant photo or drawing of what the weather looks like outside
- a ten minute cassette tape of classroom sounds

- _____
- _____

GOALS

- List two or more behavior goals or objectives for the day. (Examples: Everyone will try to say please and thank you, to wish Becky a Happy Birthday, to wait their turn, to clean their desks, etc.)

- List two or more academic goals or objectives for the day. (Examples: Everyone will try to learn to spell three new words, to finish at least one seatwork paper, to read one library book or story, to ask three different questions, etc.)

- _____

- _____

PREDICTIONS

- What will the menu be for lunch? What will taste good?
- How many classmates will be in attendance by the end of the day?
- How many seatwork papers will be completed?
- What will the weather be like by the end of the day?
- Who will win the relay race or game in P.E.?
- Divide several ice cubes between two containers (a plastic butter dish and a thermos bottle will work fine). Seal both. Predict what will happen to the ice in each container by the end of the day.
- Mix up a small amount of bread dough. (Flour, water, yeast and a little sugar.) Knead the dough and place in a container. Make close observations. Measure the height and width of the ball of dough. Weigh it. Take an instant photo or draw a picture of it. Predict what will happen to it by the end of the day.
- Make three wishes for the end of the day.

- _____

- _____

Step Two: Place all the information from above in a box. Place an alarm clock set for 2:45 p.m. inside the box. Tape the box securely and attach this label:

MINI TIME CAPSULE: DO NOT TOUCH!

DO NOT OPEN UNTIL 2:45 P.M.

Place the capsule in a secure but visible place.

Step Three: Anticipation! It is important that learners see the capsule all day but not be able to open it. Recording the time remaining until the opening of the capsule on a "Count Down Chart" is lots of fun. It's also a good math exercise.

Step Four: Ten, nine, eight, seven, six, five, four, three, two, one! The alarm goes off! It's 2:45 p.m. and time to open the **Mini Time Capsule** and examine the contents.

Discussion topics and questions:

1. Compare/contrast all the "now stuff" from the morning with the present.

2. Check on the science experiments involving the ice and bread dough. Discuss.

3. Chart the goals and predictions. Which goals were accomplished? How many predictions were correct?

4. What happened between morning and afternoon that was not predicted? Were there any surprises? (Ms. Johnson got paint on her dress. Billy fell down and skinned his knee. Kathy went home with the flu, etc.)

5. How many hours, minutes, and seconds "old" was the time capsule?

6. Did the day seem to go fast or slow? Why?

7. Lots of things didn't change at all. List them.

8. Teach the words obvious and subtle as they apply to the change process. Discuss examples.

Mini Time Capsule #2 (Five Days)

After completing the 1-day time capsule, the teacher/facilitator guides learners through another **Mini Time Capsule** experience. This time the capsule will not be opened for 5 days or one school week. Fill the capsule with "now stuff," goals and predictions using previous examples for the one-day capsule. Complete the five-day capsule experience by following steps one through four for the one-day capsule.

Fill the capsule with suggestions from the previous capsule. Additional recommendations for enclosures in a Five-Day Time Capsule:

1. Write a letter from Monday addressed to Friday.

2. Plant bean seeds in a container small enough to fit in the capsule.

3. Begin a small crystal garden.

4. Video tape lots of "Now Stuff":

. . . the first practice of a new song or dance that will be performed on Friday.

. . . the entire class learning how to juggle.

. . . the school yard and street before the trash is picked up.

. . . an empty bulletin board.

5. Collect clippings from Monday's newspaper.

6. Place several slices of raw fruit and vegetables in small containers - one sealed, one open.

7. Watch the news on CNN. Take notes.

8. _____

9. _____

10. _____

Seal, label and secure the capsule in a safe place. Repeat steps three and four using the discussion topics and questions. Compare/contrast the Five-Day Capsule with the One-Day Capsule.

Mini Time Capsule #3 (Thirty Days)

After completing the five-day capsule, continue to expand the learners' comprehension of time by guiding them through a 30-day capsule. Fill the capsule with "now stuff," goals and predictions using the examples and suggestions for the one-day and five-day capsule. Complete the 30-day capsule experience by following steps one through four for the one-day capsule.

Fill the capsule with suggestions from previous capsules. Additional recommendations for enclosures in a 30-Day Time Capsule:

1. A photo or drawing of Ms. Johnson on the first day of her new diet.

2. Photocopy several letters that were sent to legislators, school board, editor of local newspaper, mayor/city planner, director of a zoo, director of a nursing home, etc. explaining concerns of individual learners. (Compare/contrast with replies after the capsule is opened.)

3. Predict the final scores of several sporting events that will be occurring during the month.

4. Include a "now stuff" list of current events from around the community, state and world.

5. Construct party favors for an end-of-the-month time capsule party.

6. Construct a chart predicting the weather for each day of the month.

7. Take several "before" photos of people, buildings, plants, etc. (Compare/contrast with "after" photos at the end of the month.)

8. Write one or two community service goals for the month.

9. _____

10. _____

Seal, label and secure the capsule in a safe place. Repeat steps three and four using discussion topics and questions. Compare/contrast the Thirty-Day Capsule with the Five-Day and One-Day Capsules.

Mini Time Capsule #4 (One School Year)

The final Time Capsule covers an entire school year - 8 or 9 months. By now the teacher/facilitator has led learners through a progression of Mini Time Capsules, from 1 day to 30. A capsule that covers several months will offer lots of surprises on the day it is opened. The learners will be able to make significant observations and comparisons in just a few months. Fill the capsule with "now stuff," goals and predictions using examples and suggestions from the other capsules. Complete the 1-year capsule experience by following steps one through four from the one-day capsule.

Fill the capsule with suggestions from previous capsules. Additional recommendations for enclosures in a One-Year Time Capsule:

1. Samples of learners' handwriting, creative writing, grades, etc.

2. Tape recording of learners' reading and/or singing ability.

3. Learner-produced video tape.

4. Win/loss predictions for sporting events. (World Series, Super Bowl)

5. Win/loss predictions for school elections and competitions.

6. Current page number in each textbook that learners are working on.

7. Current favorite T.V. show, movie, book, food, sport, etc. for each learner.

8. Predict birthday, Christmas and/or Hanukkah gifts.

9. Yearlong physical fitness goals.

10. Yearlong community service project goals.

11. Yearlong school improvement project goals.

12. _____

13. _____

14. _____

Seal, label and secure the capsule in a safe place. Repeat steps three and four using discussion topics and questions. Compare/contrast the One-Year Capsule with the Thirty-Day, Five-Day and One-Day Capsules.

The Real Thing
A 10-Year Personal Time Capsule

IT'S ABOUT ME!

Things happen. People change. Times change. But how can we tell? A personal time capsule is a fun, exciting slice from one person's life. Learners use all their skills of creativity to personalize their capsule and make it truly unique. The capsule will not be opened for 10 years so don't rush the collection process. Encourage learners to think about the contents. The following suggestions are just that - suggestions. They are intended as motivators, to jump-start the imagination of learners as they survey the present and contemplate the future. The most important consideration for this capsule is the word personal. Learners will enjoy brainstorming ideas for the contents of the capsule with a partner, but they should also be encouraged to include observations and memorabilia that are very personal and unique to them.

Containers:

Each of the following containers has a good "track record" for durability. Think about it. Ten years is a long time! The container must be sturdy.

Plastic shoe box
Tupperwear® type container
Pringle® Potato Chips can
Two 32 oz. plastic soft drink bottles with the tops cut off and
    ends taped together
Plastic or metal lunch pail or box
Metal or plastic tackle box or tool box

Sealing the Capsule:

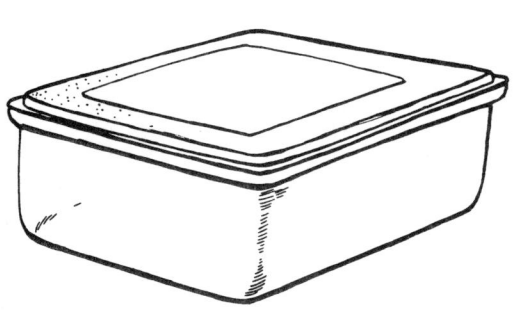

A roll of duct tape is a must. Whatever the container, it must be taped well to prevent nosy critters, both four legged and two legged, from chewing, scratching, eating or otherwise peeking inside. Moisture can be a problem. Shrink-wrapping the entire capsule would be ideal.

A clearly printed label (laminated if possible) should be secured to the outside of the capsule.

The label might look like this:

> **TIME CAPSULE**
> **Do Not Touch! Do Not Open!**
> **Do not open until January 10, 2010.**
> **This time capsule is the *personal property* of**
> **John Doe, Box 200, Creal Springs, IL. 62922**
>
> Mr. & Mrs. Robert Doe, 1000 Lake View Dr., Beavercreek, AL.
> are authorized to store this capsule until the time of opening.
>
> If this time capsule has been misplaced,
> please return it to the owner or authorized agent.

The Keeper of the Capsule:

Most time capsules are buried under the corner of a building, protected by layers of concrete and brick. The owner of the Ten-Year Capsule must find a trusted friend or family member who will accept the responsibility of storing the capsule for ten years. When the owner of the capsule is a child, one of the best "keepers" is a grandparent. Over a ten year period many things can happen - families move or parents divorce. However, grandparents go right on! They are not only loyal to their grandchildren, they take great delight in saving memorabilia. Grandparents have been known to make the opening of the capsule after ten years a great celebration, personally delivering the capsule and sharing the experience as the grandchild examines the contents.

Contents of a 10-year Time Capsule:

The contents might include, but not be limited to:

personal data form_____	pictures_____	photos_____
drawings_____	reports_____	interviews_____
magazine ad_____	computer disk_____	souvenirs_____
mementos_____	cassette tape_____	art work_____
samples of school work_____	newspaper clippings_____	video tape_____
miniature toys_____	weather report_____	schedules_____
sample pages from diary_____	photo copies of awards_____	birthday card_____
pressed flowers/leaves_____	piece of jewelry_____	_____
letter from parent_____	letter from grandparent_____	_____
_____	_____	_____

Personal Data Form

My Autobiography

(photo)

Name:_____ Date:_____

Address:_____ Phone: _____

_____

School:_____Grade:_____

IMPORTANT PEOPLE IN MY LIFE:

Parents:_____

_____ **FAVORITES:**

Family:_____ Food: _____

Teachers:_____ Song: _____

Friends:_____ Sport: _____

Others:_____ T.V. Show: _____

_____ Movie: _____

GGA2000 © Pieces of Learning

I know a sample price of various things:

Movie $_____   CD $_____

Fast Food $_____   Birthday Card $_____

This is what is happening in my life right now:

This is what is happening in my school right now:

This is what is happening in my family right now:

This is what is happening in my community right now:

This is what is happening in my state right now:

This is what is happening in the world right now:

The things that really "bug" me in my life are:

The funniest, silliest thing that ever happened to me was:

It's a "Sign of the Times." These are the SYMBOLS that depict my life and world:

These are the things I am most proud of:

My heroes are:

Drawings/Illustrations/Photos of current FADS, POPULAR FASHIONS and IDEAS:

Did you hear the one about . . ? (My favorite joke)

I HAVE MANY QUESTIONS ABOUT THE FUTURE:

1.

2.

3.

4.

GOALS AND OBJECTIVES FOR MY FUTURE:

In one year I hope
_____

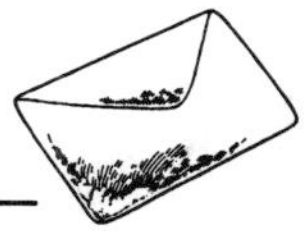

_____

In five years maybe
_____

_____

In ten years it would really be great if
_____

_____

A wonderful surprise for my family in the future would be _____

_____

The best thing that could happen for the world is _____

_____

If I could change one thing in my life it would be _____

_____

_____

Three promises I will try to keep are:

1.

2.

3.

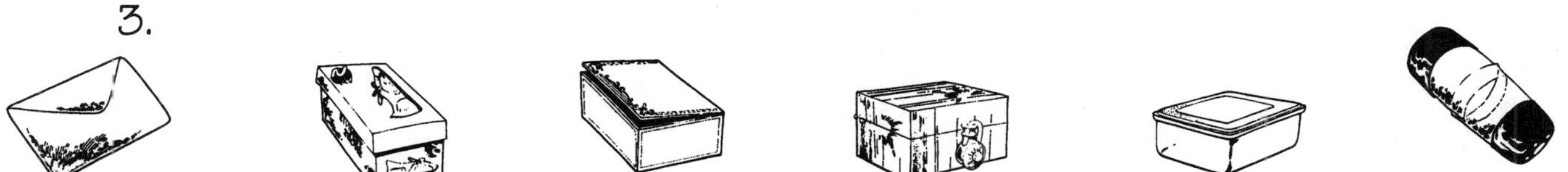

Two people I will try to do special things for are:

 1.

2.

 A Drawing/Illustration/Photo of a gift I would like to give the world:

 **PREDICTIONS FOR THE FUTURE:**

I predict that _____ will win the _____.

I predict that _____ will cost _____.

I predict that _____ will change from _____ to _____.

I predict that I will be _____ because _____.

I predict my best friend will _____.

I predict my parents will _____.

A Letter To The Future From ME!

Dear _____ ,

Date: (10 years from now)

_____

_____

_____

_____

_____

_____

_____

_____

_____

_____

_____

_____

_____

From: _____

Current Date: _____

As a former classroom teacher, the author has enjoyed receiving letters from former learners about their time capsules. When learners opened their capsules after ten years, they found the following letter:

Dear _____
(Learner's name)

WOW! You made it! Congratulations! Ten years have gone by. I hope you are having lots of fun looking through your time capsule. Please write and let me know what happened. Tell me what surprised you most. What made you laugh? What made you sad? Was anything really weird or confusing?

Tell me about yourself now. What's going on in your life? Send photos. I look forward to hearing from you.

Yours truly,

_____
(Teacher's Signature)

Address:

A Summer Vacation Time Capsule

Some Vacation Capsules are about vacations that have already happened; a collection of memories about a trip or visit. However, this Vacation Capsule is for a vacation that hasn't happened yet. It is an "active" capsule, filled with ideas, information and fun stuff to be experienced during an entire 3-month summer break from school. Learners assemble their capsules during the last week of school. Part of the contents are consumable while other parts are completed and saved to be shared at the beginning of the next school year with old friends, new friends and new teachers.

Note: Guide learners through the planning process. Do not encourage them to organize and plan every single day of their summer vacation. Unrealistic goals only lead to disappointment, frustration and failure.

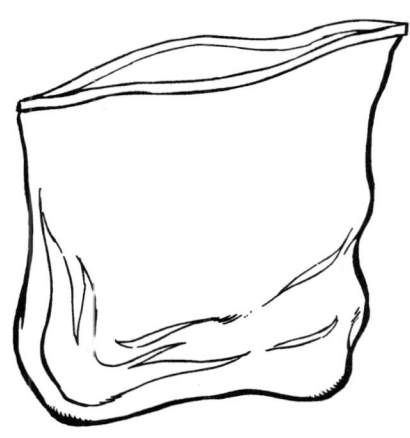

Capsule Container:

The size of the container depends on how much "stuff" each learner collects for his/her capsule. They usually start with a small box but switch to something larger, like a back pack, as they get more ideas. The switching process will probably repeat itself several times before the capsule is completed.

Contents Checklist:

"Who's Bored?" chart_____

favorite music: C.D.'s & cassettes_____

books_____   stationery_____

stamps_____   pen/pencil/markers_____

magazines_____   sun block_____

blank cassettes_____   drawing paper_____

Diary/journal_____   public library card_____

water bottle_____   sun glasses_____

3-month calendar_____

addresses/phone numbers_____

WHO'S BORED? NOT ME!
100 great ideas for summer

To the learner: Hang the following idea chart on your bedroom wall. Mark an "X" on each one as you complete them over the summer. Do you think you will complete all 100? Make a photo copy of the chart for a friend and have a contest to see who completes the most. Keep score. If you do something more than once give yourself an extra point. Add your own ideas. Good Luck! Have a great summer!

1. Write a letter to you-know-who about you-know-what.
2. Do a chore for a family member without being asked.
3. Read a book.
4. Go swimming.
5. Call Grandma and Grandpa.
6. Celebrate_____'s birthday.
7. Go shopping.
8. Write a poem or story about a dragon named Douglas who came for a visit.
9. Draw a picture. Include it in a letter to Grandma.
10. Ride a bike.
11. Play a board game with friends and family.
12. Ask a friend to be a summer pen pal. Write every week.
13. Compose a RAP about funny things people do.

14. Go outside, look up at the sky and find animal shapes in the clouds. Draw pictures of them.
15. Listen to music.
16. Play baseball.
17. Create a nice surprise for Mom and Dad.
18. Tape record yourself reading a story or singing a song.
19. Have a picnic.

20. Create a "Back To School" checklist of things to do and things to get before school starts.
21. Go on a trip with your family.
22. Play soccer.
23. Send a joke to the Rosie O'Donnell T.V. Show.
24. Sit in the backyard and dream about an imaginary trip to Disney World.
25. Create a plan for correcting a bad habit.
26. Plant some flowers.

27. Use a tape measure, ruler or yardstick to measure lots of "stuff" in your home. Keep a list.
28. Help cook dinner.
29. Celebrate a holiday.
30. Read another book
31. Read two magazines.
32. Write a letter to a favorite sports star.
33. Go to the public library and check out three books.
34. Listen to some new music.
35. Wash the car.
36. Go skateboarding.
37. Play a new game on the computer.
38. Find ten strange words in the newspaper. Write their definitions and learn how to spell them.
39. Take back library books before they are overdue.
40. Have a slumber party for friends.
41. Be extra nice to a brother or sister.
42. Organize family photos and put them in albums.
43. Go to the zoo.
44. Compliment Mom on her appearance.
45. Jog around the neighborhood.
46. Surf the Internet with an adult.
47. Go to camp.
48. Add money to your piggy bank for a new_____.
49. Clean your bedroom closet.
50. Look through old photograph albums with Nanna.
51. Invite a friend over for pizza and videos.
52. Organize your collection of_____.
53. Help Mom or Dad with the yard work.
54. Make a dental appointment before school starts.
55. Organize a neighborhood checkers or chess tournament.
56. Have a jump rope contest with two friends.
57. Stay overnight at a cousin's house.
58. Build a cardboard clubhouse in the backyard.
59. Get a haircut.
60. Practice cheers with three friends.
61. Write a play and perform it for friends and family.
62. Return all the "stuff" that you borrowed from_____.
63. Send an E-Mail to you-know-who.
64. Create a budget for your allowance for the next three months
65. Work out with Mom using an exercise video.
66. Write a letter to_____at summer camp.
67. Collect newspapers and aluminum cans to take to a recycling center.

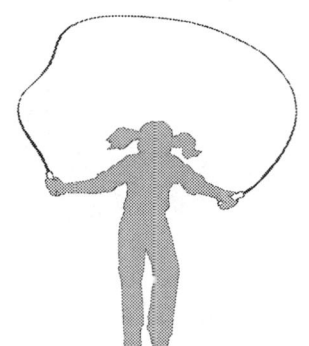

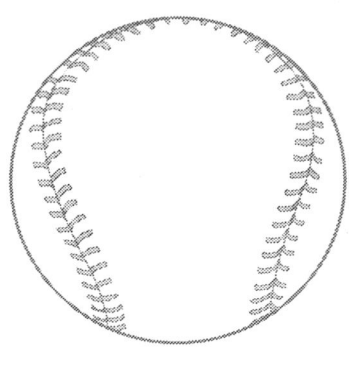

68. Go to an amusement park with your family.
69. Go to a sports camp.
70. Rearrange the furniture in your bedroom.
71. Read another book.
72. Negotiate an increase in your allowance.
73. Go to work with Dad or Mom.
74. Give Mom a back rub.
75. Buy a white tee shirt and decorate it with magic markers.
76. Write a letter to the President of the United States.
77. Invite two friends over to play in the sprinkler in the backyard.
78. Set up a lemonade stand in the front yard.

79. Gather old clothes from your family and donate them to Good Will.
80. Make a bunch of crazy inventions out of junk.
81. Play cards with a senior citizen.
82. Have a wiener roast.
83. Ask parents and grandparents for recipes and make a personal recipe book.
84. Don't watch television for 48 hours.
85. Draw your family tree.
86. Take your bike to the police station and get a safety check.
87. Make mud pies.
88. Switch bedrooms with a brother or sister.
89. Design a personal coat-of-arms and hang it on your bedroom door.
90. Give the dog a bath.
91. Design and make your own personal address book.
92. Write a story about a monster that lives in the garage.
93. Clean out the garage — including the monster.

94. Go to a travel agency and ask for free travel posters to hang in your room.
95. Go to the bank and open a savings account.
96. Design and make several miniature Styrofoam boats to sail in the bathtub.
97. Ask Grandpa to teach you how to make change.
98. Start getting up earlier so your "body clock" is ready for the first day of school.
99. Organize a family fire drill. Practice three times!
100. Read one more book.

Another important part of the Vacation Capsule is keeping a 3-Month Calendar. Learners fill in the blank calendar with birthdays, anniversaries, celebrations and special events scheduled for the summer. They may also add photos, drawings, magazine pictures, illustrations and other ideas to personalize their calendars.

JUNE

Sunday	Monday	Tuesday	Wednesday	Thursday	Friday	Saturday

JULY

Sunday	Monday	Tuesday	Wednesday	Thursday	Friday	Saturday

AUGUST

Sunday	Monday	Tuesday	Wednesday	Thursday	Friday	Saturday

A Living Time Capsule

Grandparents, great-grandparents and other senior citizens are true examples of living time capsules. Their life experiences span several decades and offer wonderful opportunities for young learners to understand how things change. Through story telling, oral history, photo albums, scrapbooks, knickknacks and other memorabilia a grandchild can gently pry open a treasury filled with lessons from life and personal values. Let's face it, kids are nosy! And curiosity is a great motivator in the learning process.

An interview with grandparents should be relaxed, informal and fun. Grandchildren can record questions and answers using audio tapes. Go slow! Three short interviews are better than one long one. Consider sharing some of the questions ahead of time so grandparents have a chance to think about their responses. If grandparents live too far away for a personal interview, learners can use the U.S. mail or E-mail to communicate.

Joe Wayman begins his book, **If You Promise Not To Tell**, with the poem CORNERS. It is a perfect beginning for opening a living time capsule.

CORNERS

May I share a little corner,
Of my life, just one or two?
Perhaps they'll seem familiar,
As if you had lived them too.

If our corners seem a bit alike,
Then just perhaps it's true:
You're a little bit like me,
And I'm a little bit like you.

From **If You Promise Not To Tell**
Written & illustrated by
Joe Wayman
Pieces of Learning
Dayton, Ohio 1991

Begin by filling in a family tree—together!

My Family Tree

Sample Family Tree

Grandpa & Grandma tell me about....

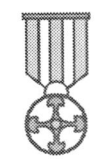

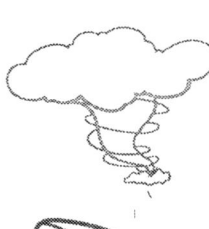

....one of your heroes.
....your favorite T.V. Show.
....all the paying jobs and careers you have had in your life.
....the awards, honors or prizes you have won.
....the best part of being a grandparent.
....the price of groceries when you were a kid.
....the happiest time in your life.
....your favorite teacher in school.
....your favorite teacher who was not a school teacher.
....a big mess you made when you were a kid.
....your grandma and grandpa.
....the Vietnam War.
....a famous person you once met.
....the first time you drove a car.
....your best friend.
....the time you got hurt.
....a place you always wanted to visit but never did.
....a disappointment you had.
....the toughest job you ever had.
....the time you got caught in bad weather.
....the smartest thing you ever did.
....the time you saved somebody's life.
....a time when you were really afraid.
....the nicest gift someone gave you.

....that time when you really felt proud.
....the time you realized you needed to ask for help.
....your favorite vacation.
....the clubs and organizations you belong to.
....your favorite pets.
....a sport you always wanted to play professionally.
....the time you almost got killed.
....the meaning of the words old fashioned.
....a time when you were being too stubborn.
....an invention that changed your life.
....a holiday celebration that was the most fun.
....your favorite songs.
....the time you lost your temper.
....a time when you almost lost hope.
....your favorite photographs.
....things that have changed the most in your life.
....things that make you angry in your community.
....your plans for the future.
....how tomorrow can be better than yesterday.
....something new and different you want to learn to do.

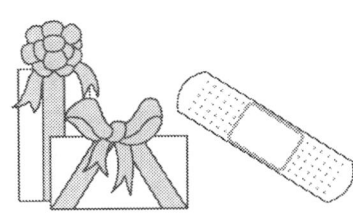
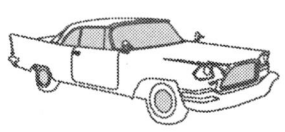

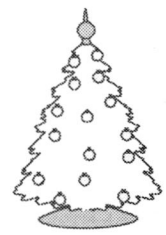

Capsules—and MORE Capsules!

Space Capsule: Create a special time capsule about earth that will be sent into outer space to be found by _____? The capsule can be no bigger than a shoe box. What things should be included? What things should be left out?

The Traveling Capsule: One learner begins a capsule (any topic) and passes it along to another learner, class or school. Each person adds "new stuff," goals and predictions.

Sports Capsule: This specialized capsule includes current stats, clippings, pictures, interviews, and other data about a favorite sport. Be sure to include the history of the sport plus some predictions about its future popularity.

The "Guess Who?" Capsule: Research the life and times of a famous person. Fill the capsule with clues about the person. What effect will this person's life have on the future? Learners trade finished capsules, study the clues and guess the name of the person.

Our School: This is the real thing.
(1) Establish a "Time Capsule Planning Committee" (one learner from each grade level plus faculty/parent sponsors and representatives from the local historical society) to organize the gathering of information, data and materials. (2) Establish committees for selecting and obtaining the container, locating and gaining permission for the burial site, and handling PR and press releases.

Invent a new "junk" food.

A Computer Capsule:
Done entirely on the computer, using any topic or theme, this capsule ends up on a disk. With adult supervision, learners surf the Internet for their information. How about a computer capsule about computers?

The Mystery Capsule:
This capsule contains clues about a school, town, city, county, state or country. The people who open the capsule guess the location. A mystery capsule could also be filled with clues about a famous person, book, document, event or time in history.

A Food Capsule:
Gather magazine pictures, drawings and illustrations of current popular foods. Create several sample menus using different ethnic foods. Include lots of recipes.

Teacher Time Capsules:
Principal leads his/her staff through the time capsule process at the first staff meeting in the fall. They write "now stuff," goals and predictions on a piece of paper and seal it up in an envelope addressed to themselves. The principal mails it back to them at the end of the school year.

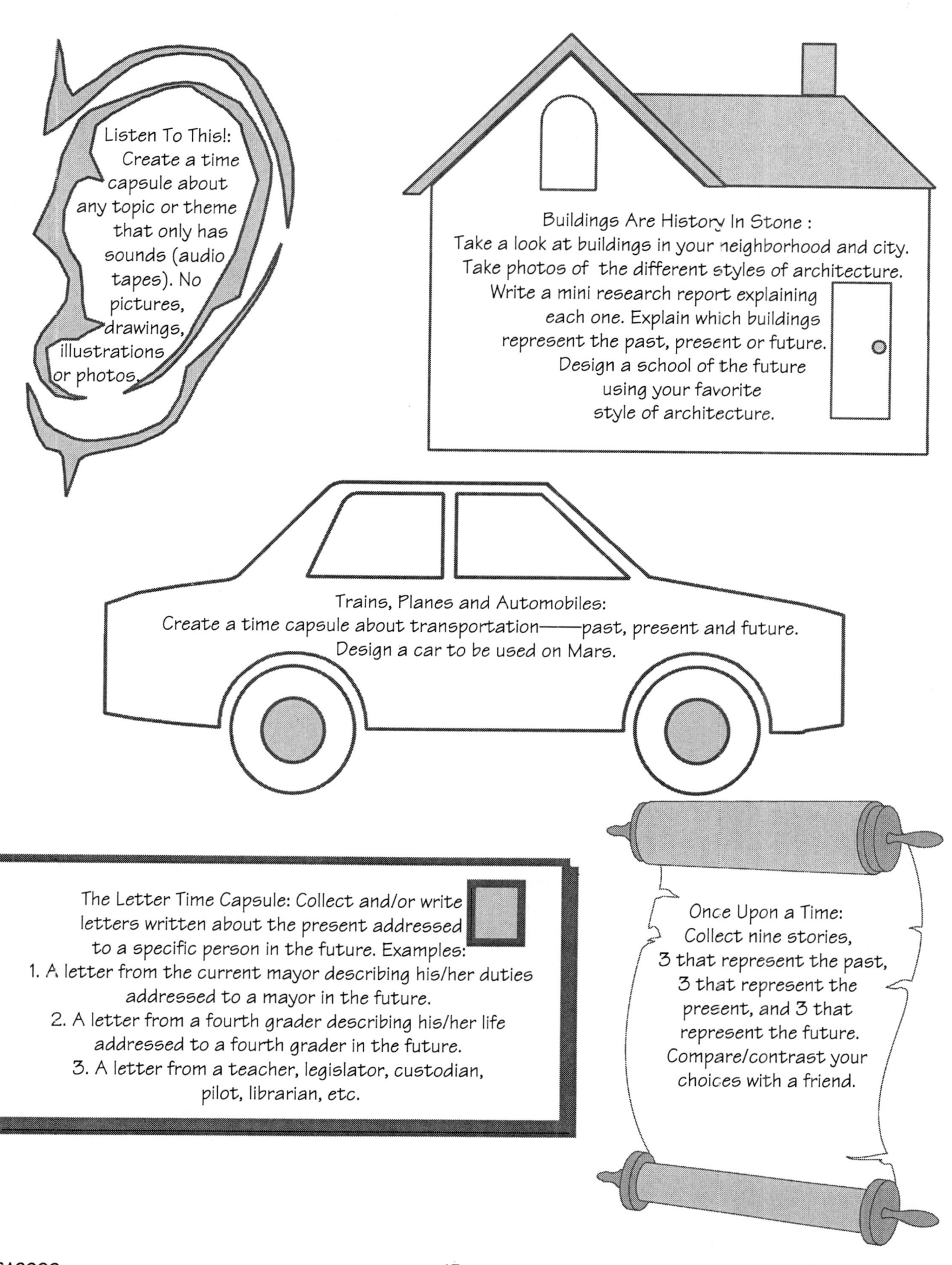

The Empty Capsule:
Examine this capsule very closely. Since this capsule is empty, all the clues for the missing contents are written or painted on the outside of the container. It's a mystery! Good Luck in finding the missing contents.

The Question Capsule:
Compose a list a questions you would like to ask the "future." Compose a list of questions the "future" might like to ask you.

Look Closer!
Create a time capsule about any topic or theme that only has pictures, photos, drawings and illustrations. NO WORDS!

Math Time Capsule:
Learners research the history of math including data on famous mathematicians. They also survey and gather examples of current math usage in their home, school, community and world. The math capsule is filled with examples of math "stuff."

One BIG Time Capsule:
Build a plastic bubble big enough to hold 20 people. Inflate the bubble using an electric fan and fill it with "now stuff," goal/objectives, predictions, symbols and other information about the rain forest. Invite other classes to come and visit your bubble. Keep the bubble and change the theme each month.

Activities—and MORE Activities!

1. While digging in your backyard you find a time capsule. Write about it. What's in it? Who placed it there? Why? What could you add to bring it up to date?

2. The local police department finds a time capsule in the form of an old filing cabinet that contains clues to an unsolved crime. What was the crime? What are the clues? Pretend you are a journalist and you solve the mystery. Write about it.

3. You have just been appointed chairperson for the National Time Capsule Bureau. You must publish a set of guidelines that each state must use to create a time capsule for the new century.

4. Teacher/facilitator buries a time capsule on the property of the school. Learners dig up the capsule, discuss and write about what they find. The capsule may be about a place, event, time in history or famous person.

5. Cooperative group activity: Each member of the group does a different kind of capsule about the same subject or idea and then they compare/contrast the finished capsules. Types of capsules: visual, sounds, words, objects, questions, letters, etc.

6. Create a micro-mini capsule about yourself. It can only contain three sentences, three objects, and three pictures. Choose carefully! Will your friends be able to tell that it is a capsule about you?

7. Guess the future. Create an imaginary capsule compiled by a citizen of the United States in the year 3000. The capsule will be opened 100 years later. You can only imagine what might be in it!

8. Alphabet Capsules: Create an "All About The Letter "A" Time Capsule," "All About The Letter "B" Time Capsule," etc. Include pictures, symbols and small objects whose names begin with the same letter.

9. A hunting we will go! Go on a hunt for REAL time capsules buried in your town, city or county. County and state historical societies are good places to start.

10. Have a "Let's Time It!" day. Use a stop watch, alarm clock, hour glass and sun dial. Brainstorm a list of things to time. Chart the results.

The very best time capsule ever...

It takes awhile to recover from the death of a parent. It was six months before I felt comfortable enough to start sorting through all the "stuff" in the basement. But I knew it was time. My Dad didn't need to be stumbling over boxes of what I thought at the time might be painful memories. My aunts volunteered to help, but something or someone told me it should be a private task.

My Mom was truly a renaissance woman - in every sense of the word. She had so many passions throughout her life and relished all the roles she played: daughter, sister, wife, mother, friend, neighbor, hostess, mentor, confidant, homemaker, farmer, store clerk, published poet, artist, gourmet cook, professional floral arranger, historian, gardener, bookkeeper, 4-H leader, Sunday school director, teacher's aide, champion fisherman, fund raiser for charities, political activist, swimming instructor, and officer in countless clubs and organizations. She was a smart, strong-willed woman with a tender, generous heart.

My Mom was also a saver. It was just not in her nature to throw anything away. I must have heard her say a hundred times, "Well, we better keep that. You never know when it might come in handy." In 1956 when my Dad began making plans to build our new home, it was stylish to have only half basements under houses. But he knew better! There would have to be a full basement under Verna Frances Johnson. And over the years, that full basement - filled up!

On every shelf, in every corner, under every table, in every box there were pieces of her. An autobiography of "stuff." A personal time capsule left by a lifelong learner. Like pieces of a puzzle, each object I touched brought me a fuller, richer, more complete picture of my mother. Scrapbooks, clothes, commemorative dishes, vacation souvenirs, photos, artificial flowers, holiday decorations, books, letters, recipe books, fishing equipment, craft supplies, canning jars, tools, quilt tops, baskets and flower vases. So many vases! Where on earth did she get all those vases? On and on, piece by piece, the puzzle came together. Memories and surprises. Old questions answered, new questions asked. Symbols, frozen in time, from a life of 58 years. Through the laughter and the tears I made my way through the treasury, first wishing she could have been there with me and then realizing - she was. Thank you, Dad, for building that full basement.

Into my heart's treasury I slipped a coin,
That time cannot take nor a thief purloin.
Oh better than the minting of a gold crowned king,
Is the safe kept memory of a lovely thing   - Sara Teasdale

Verna Frances Johnson   June 21, 1917 - April 3, 1976

TO NETWORK WITH THESE 21ST CENTURY USERS

Learners...

...who are curious about the new millennium.
...who need help understanding the relationship between the past, present and future.
...who need practice working in cooperative groups.
...who like to have fun with ideas.

Teachers...

...who need thematic-based, innovative curriculum.
...who need motivating activities that stimulate thinking and creativity in learners.
...who are themselves life-long learners interested in new ideas and concepts.

Parents/Grandparents...

...who enjoy learning with their children/grandchildren.
...who need at-home learning experiences that explore the past, present and future.
...who want a creative way to share past experiences and memories with their children/grandchildren.

Home schoolers...

...who need practical, inexpensive, easy-to-assemble learning activities.
...who enjoy involving other family members in the study of history.
...who want to help children develop attitudes of optimism and hope about the future.

Administrators/Supervisors of Curriculum...

...who want to show leadership in the development of creative curriculum.
...who need curriculum that fits various teaching styles.
...who need independent study activities for gifted/talented learners.
...who want flexible curriculum easily adaptable to different grade levels.
...who need activities for at-risk learners in an inclusive classroom.

The Rosary

The Gospel on Beads for Grades 2–6

Imprimatur:
Most Rev. Gerald F. Kicanas, Bishop of Tucson

The Nihil Obstat and the Imprimatur are a declaration that a book is considered free from doctrinal or moral error. It is not implied that those who have granted the Nihil Obstat and Imprimatur agree with the contents, opinions or statements expressed.

Scripture texts in this work are excerpts from the *New American Bible with Revised New Testament and Psalms* Copyright © 1991, 1986, 1970 Confraternity of Christian Doctrine, Inc., Washington, D.C. Used with permission. All rights reserved. No portion of the *New American Bible* may be reprinted without permission in writing from the copyright holder.

THE BOOK TEAM
- Ernie Nedder, Publisher
- Kathy Nedder, CFO
- Sister Mary Kathleen Glavich, SND, Author and Illustrator
- Rev. Thomas M. Santa, CSsR, Theological Editor
- Kate Harrison, Editor
- Lone Quail Media, Design Services
    Jolene Campbell, Designer

Copyright © 2004
E.T. Nedder Publishing
All rights reserved.

Except for the reproducible Masters, no part of this book may be reprinted or transmitted in any form or by any means, electronic or mechanical, or by an information retrieval system, without permission in writing from the publisher. Reproducible pages are for single classroom use only.

Additional copies of this publication may be purchased by sending check or money order for $15 to: Theological Book Service, P.O. Box 509, Barnhart, MO 63012. Or call toll free 1-888-247-3023.
Fax: 1-800-325-9526. E-mail: bookstore@theobooks.org. Be sure to check our Web site for a list of other products: www.nedderpublishing.com.

Order # 39-0
8 1/2 x 11

Individual copies: $15.
Multiple copy discounts available.

ISBN: 1-893757-39-0

Table of Contents

Introduction

The Rosary	1
Rosary Acrostic	2
Rosary Arithmetic	2
Where to Pray the Prayers	3
The Apostles' Creed	4
The Our Father	5
The Hail Mary	6
The Doxology	7
Prayers to End the Rosary	8
Our Lady of the Rosary: Fatima	9
Prayers for the Rosary	10
When to Pray the Rosary	11
The Mysteries of the Rosary	12

Joyful Mysteries

The Annunciation	13
The Visitation	14
The Nativity	15
The Presentation	16
The Finding in the Temple	17

Luminous Mysteries

The Baptism of Jesus	18
The Wedding in Cana	19
Proclamation of the Good News	20
The Transfiguration	21
The Institution of the Eucharist	22

Sorrowful Mysteries

The Agony in the Garden	23
The Scourging at the Pillar	24
The Crowning with Thorns	25
The Carrying of the Cross	26
The Crucifixion and Death of Jesus	27

Glorious Mysteries

The Resurrection	28
The Ascension	29
The Coming of the Holy Spirit	30
The Assumption of Mary	31
The Crowning of Mary	32

Flashcards of the Mysteries	33-36
Answer Key	37-39

Introduction for Parents and Teachers

The Rosary is a prayer unique to Catholics, perhaps because Catholics have a unique devotion to Mary, the Mother of God. Although people of various religions have used beads to tally prayers, we Catholics are known for our particular love for the Rosary. We give rosaries as First Communion gifts, hang them from our car mirrors, wear them, and sometimes are buried holding them in our hands. Until the Second Vatican Council, at Mass while the priest prayed in Latin, Catholics prayed the Rosary. Now that the Mass is in English and we better understand our role in the liturgy, we no longer pray the Rosary at Mass. Nevertheless, we still treasure the Rosary as a powerful prayer whether prayed alone or with others.

This booklet introduces children to the Rosary. It teaches them that the Rosary combines two forms of prayers. When we pray the Rosary, we say the words of traditional prayers: the Apostles' Creed, the Our Father, the Hail Mary, and the Doxology. At the same time we meditate on the mysteries — events in the lives of Jesus and Mary. For this reason the Rosary has been called an epitome of the Gospel. This title is even more accurate since 2002, when Pope John Paul II added the Luminous Mysteries (or Mysteries of Light) to the Joyful, Sorrowful, and Glorious Mysteries.

Activities in this booklet help the children learn the traditional prayers by heart and understand the mysteries. A page is devoted to each mystery and contains a brief explanation, activities, and a short prayer related to that mystery.

Use of Flashcards

To make flashcards from pages 33–36, photocopy Page 33 back-to-back with Page 34 and Page 35 back-to-back with page 36, using heavy paper stock. Or copy the pages on regular paper, cut out the cards and glue them onto pieces of cardboard or heavier-weight paper back-to-back so that the picture is on one side and its identification on the other. Flashcards can be used in the following ways to teach children the Mysteries in order:

- Mix the cards and have the child arrange them in the four groups of mysteries in order.

- Show the cards one by one and ask the child to identify which mystery it belongs to.

- Show each card and have the child name the mystery that comes before and after it, if there is one.

- Show a card and ask the child to tell something about the mystery.

The Rosary at Home and in School

To encourage the children to pray the Rosary, parents might begin the practice of praying the family Rosary, if they do not already do so. Teachers might pray decades of the Rosary in class. They might also plan and carry out a Living Rosary in October or May. For this devotion children, teachers, and parents representing the beads pray their respective prayer at a microphone and then set a rose or a vigil light before a statue of Mary.

By teaching our children to pray the Rosary, we pass on to them our Catholic heritage. More important, we foster devotion to Mary, God's mother and ours. Above all, because the Rosary involves reflecting on Gospel events, we help children deepen their relationship with Jesus.

The Rosary

The Rosary, a circle of beads, is a favorite Catholic prayer and very powerful. Its name comes from a word that means "rose garden." The Rosary is like a garland (a wreath) of roses because the prayers we pray on it are like roses we give to Mary, the Mother of God. By praying the Rosary, we praise God, obtain favors, and become holy.

Why do we want to give roses to Mary?
■ Write a few reasons on the card.

To Mary because

The Rosary is a two-in-one prayer. We pray with our voices and with our minds. While we pray Our Fathers and Hail Marys on the beads, we think about events in the lives of Jesus and Mary. To see what these events are called, write the letter of the alphabet that comes before each letter in the spaces provided below:

__ __ __ __ __ __ __ __ __
N Z T U F S J F T

The beads on the Rosary are in sets of ten. To find out what these sets are called, write the letter before each of these letters:

__ __ __ __ __ __ __
E F D B E F T

Rosary Acrostic

Write the key words on the lines so that the letters spell "Rosary" going down:

Key words	decades ◆ rose ◆ mysteries ◆ Mary ◆ prayer ◆ beads

__ __ **R** __
__ **O** __ __
__ __ __ **S** __
__ __ **A** __
__ __ __ **R** __ __
__ __ __ **Y** __

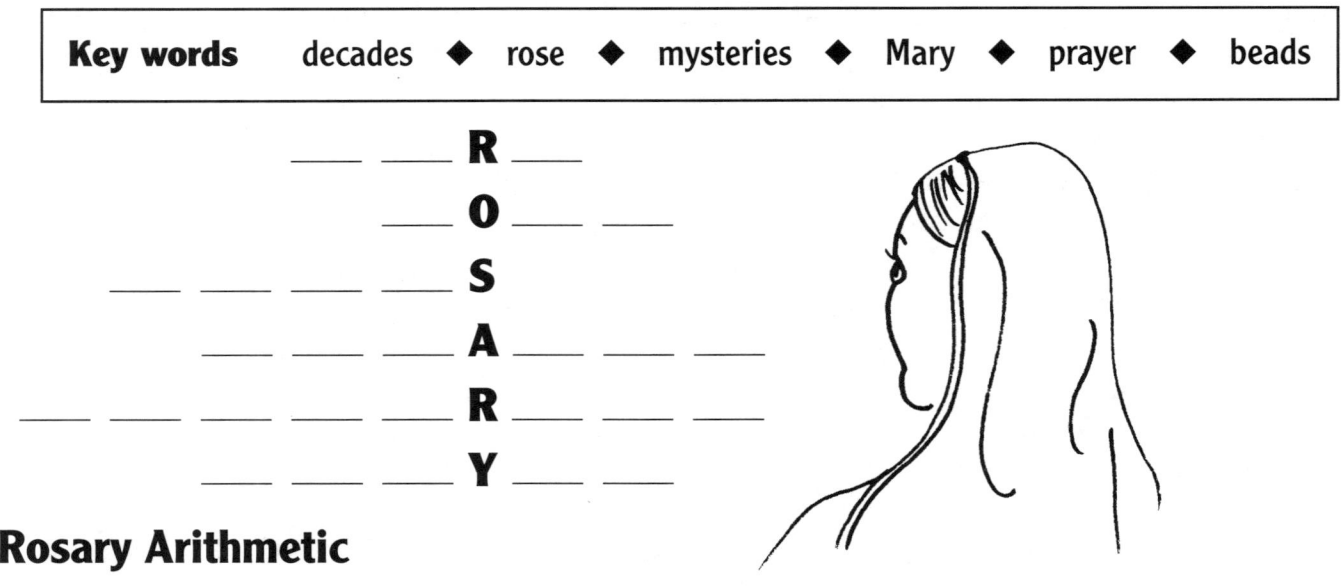

Rosary Arithmetic

1. The Rosary began in the 12th century. Write the year it is now: __ __ __ __
Subtract 1200 from this year to see about how old the Rosary is: − 1 2 0 0
_____

2. Long ago many people could not read. They couldn't pray the daily Church prayer, which includes the 150 psalms. Psalms are prayers from the Book of Psalms in the Bible. People began praying instead 150 Our Fathers on beads and later 150 Hail Marys. How many decades is 150? _____

3. Soon people began praying three sets of five mysteries each. This Rosary had one-third of the original 150 Hail Marys. How many is this? _____

4. According to a legend, in the 15th century Mary appeared to a man and told him to teach people to pray the Rosary. The religious order that this saint began promoted the Rosary. Write the numbered letter of the alphabet to find his name and the name of his religious order.

SAINT __ __ __ __ __ __ __
     4 15 13 9 14 9 3

Founder of the __ __ __ __ __ __ __ __ __ __
        4 15 13 9 14 9 3 1 13 19

Reproducible for classroom use only. Copyright © 2004 E.T. Nedder Publishing

Where to Pray the Prayers

On each large bead pray an Our Father. Color these beads red.
On each small bead pray a Hail Mary. Color these beads blue.
After each decade pray the Doxology. Put a yellow ✶ where you pray this.

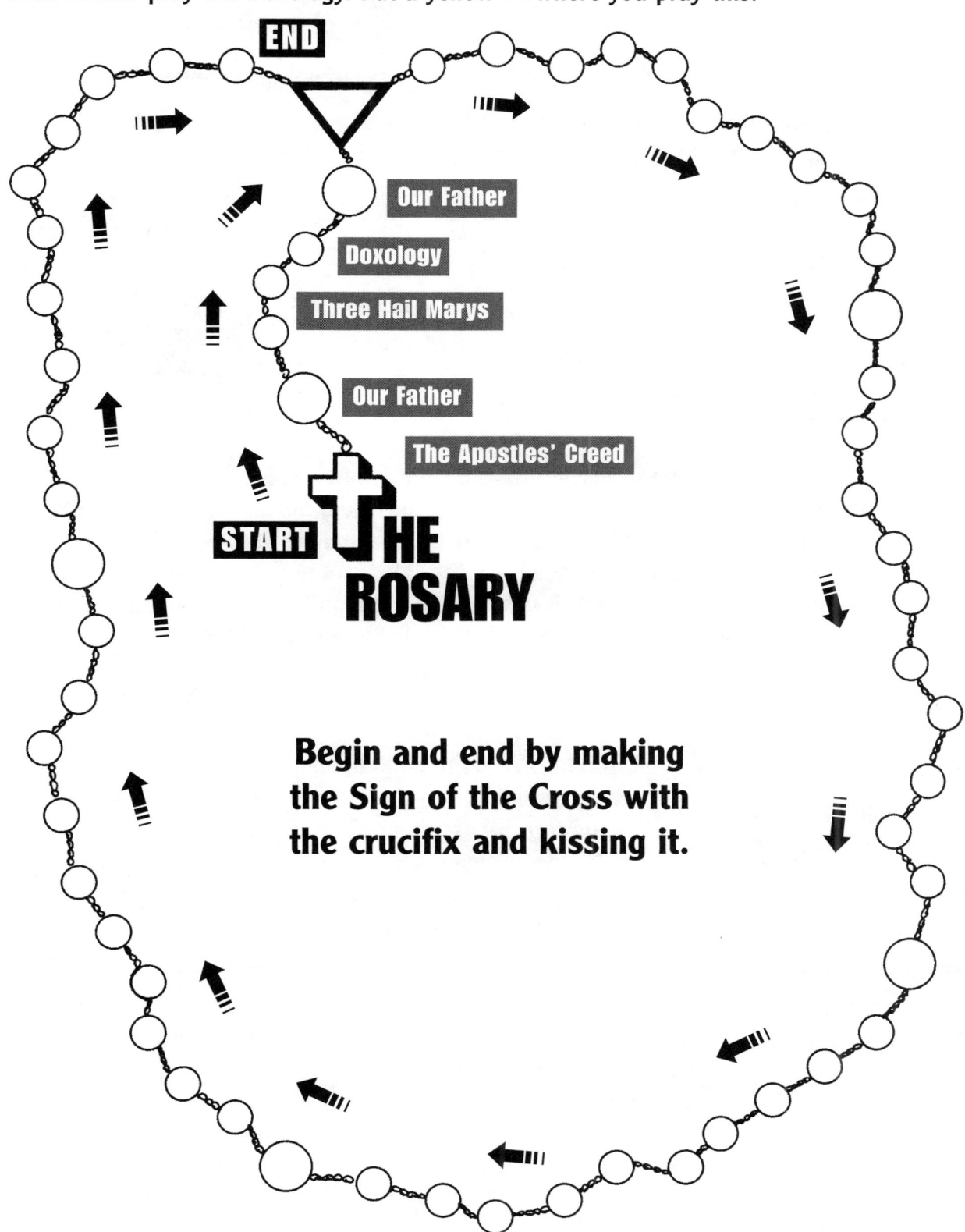

Begin and end by making the Sign of the Cross with the crucifix and kissing it.

The Apostles' Creed

We begin the Rosary by making the Sign of the Cross with the crucifix:

 In the name of the Father, and of the Son, and of the Holy Spirit. Amen.

Then we pray the Apostles' Creed on the crucifix. This Creed is one of our oldest prayers.
It states what Catholics have believed since the time of the apostles.

I believe in God,
the Father almighty,
creator of heaven
and earth.

I believe in Jesus Christ, his only Son, our Lord.
He was conceived by the power of the Holy Spirit and born of the Virgin Mary.
He suffered under Pontius Pilate, was crucified, died, and was buried.
He descended to the dead. On the third day he rose again.
He ascended into heaven and is seated at the right hand of the Father.
He will come again to judge the living and the dead.

I believe in
the Holy Spirit,
the holy catholic Church,
the communion of saints,
the forgiveness of sins,
the resurrection
of the body
and the life everlasting.

Amen.

■ Trace over the letters below that tell what "creed" means.

■ Color the pictures that match the three parts when you know each part by heart.

■ Color the cross lightly when you know the whole prayer.

Reproducible for classroom use only. Copyright © 2004 E.T. Nedder Publishing

The Our Father

When the apostles asked Jesus, "Lord, teach us to pray," he gave us the Our Father. Another name for this prayer is the Lord's Prayer. The early Christians prayed this Our Father three times a day. We pray it during Mass.

■ Find the explanation of each line in the right-hand column. Write its letter in the box.

1. Our Father, who art in heaven,
2. Hallowed be thy name.
3. Thy kingdom come
4. Thy will be done on earth as it is in heaven.
5. Give us this day our daily bread
6. And forgive us our trespasses as we forgive those who trespass against us.
7. And lead us not into temptation
8. But deliver us from evil. Amen.

A. When we sin, forgive us the way we forgive people who hurt us.
B. You, Our Creator, love and care for all of us.
C. Save us from danger in this world and the next.
D. Let us not go by persons, places or things that would make us sin.
E. May your name be holy.
F. May your justice and peace rule the world.
G. Today give us what we need to live: food and the Eucharist.
H. May people act as you know is best.

■ Jesus said that our good Father who cares for birds and flowers cares even more for us (Luke 12:22–32). In the boxes draw a bird, a flower, and yourself:

Reproducible for classroom use only. Copyright © 2004 E.T. Nedder Publishing

The Hail Mary

The Hail Mary has three parts. The first part is the words of the Angel Gabriel when he came to Mary to announce Jesus' coming. Another part was spoken by Elizabeth to Mary when Mary came to help her during her pregnancy. The last part was composed by the Church.

■ Draw a line from each part of the Hail Mary to the picture that matches it.

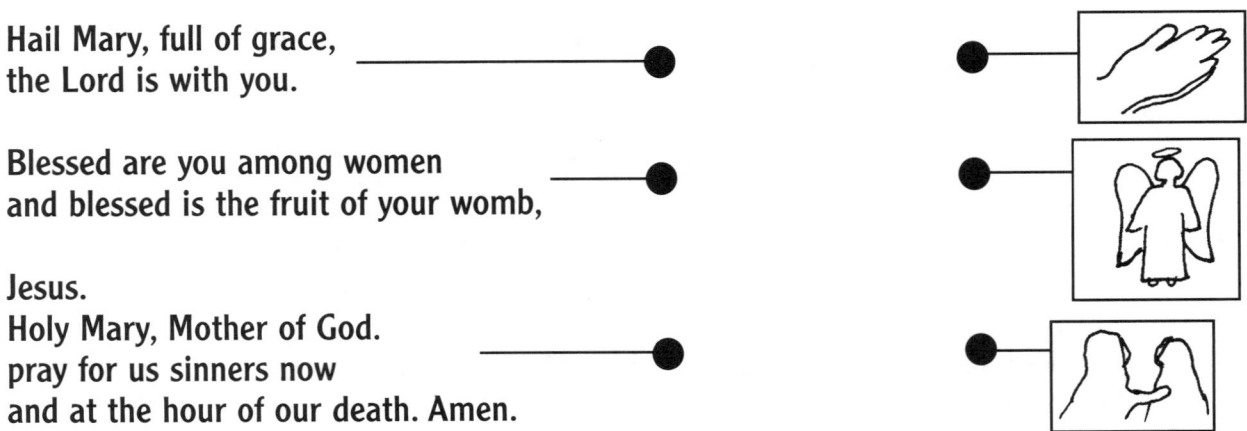

Hail Mary, full of grace,
the Lord is with you.

Blessed are you among women
and blessed is the fruit of your womb,

Jesus.
Holy Mary, Mother of God.
pray for us sinners now
and at the hour of our death. Amen.

Mary always did what God wanted. She will help you be like her. You might make a habit of praying three Hail Marys each night before you go to bed.

■ Check what God wants you to do. Write one way you will do God's will today.

God's Wish List

- ☐ Obey your mom and dad
- ☐ Eat healthy food
- ☐ Stay up late
- ☐ Tell the truth
- ☐ Give to the poor
- ☐ Help others
- ☐ Take things if you won't get caught
- ☐ Be kind to your brothers and sisters
- ☐ Bully others
- ☐ Share with others
- ☐ Take care of your things
- ☐ Pray every day
- ☐ Take dangerous dares
- ☐ Go to Sunday Mass

My Response

_____
_____
_____
_____

The Doxology

After each decade of the Rosary we pray a prayer praising the Trinity called the doxology.

■ Unscramble the missing words and write them on the lines.

Glory

to the _____, and to the _____
         ehaFte   nSo

and to the _____
        yHlo tiiprS

as it was in the beginning,

is _____, and will be forever.
    own

Amen.

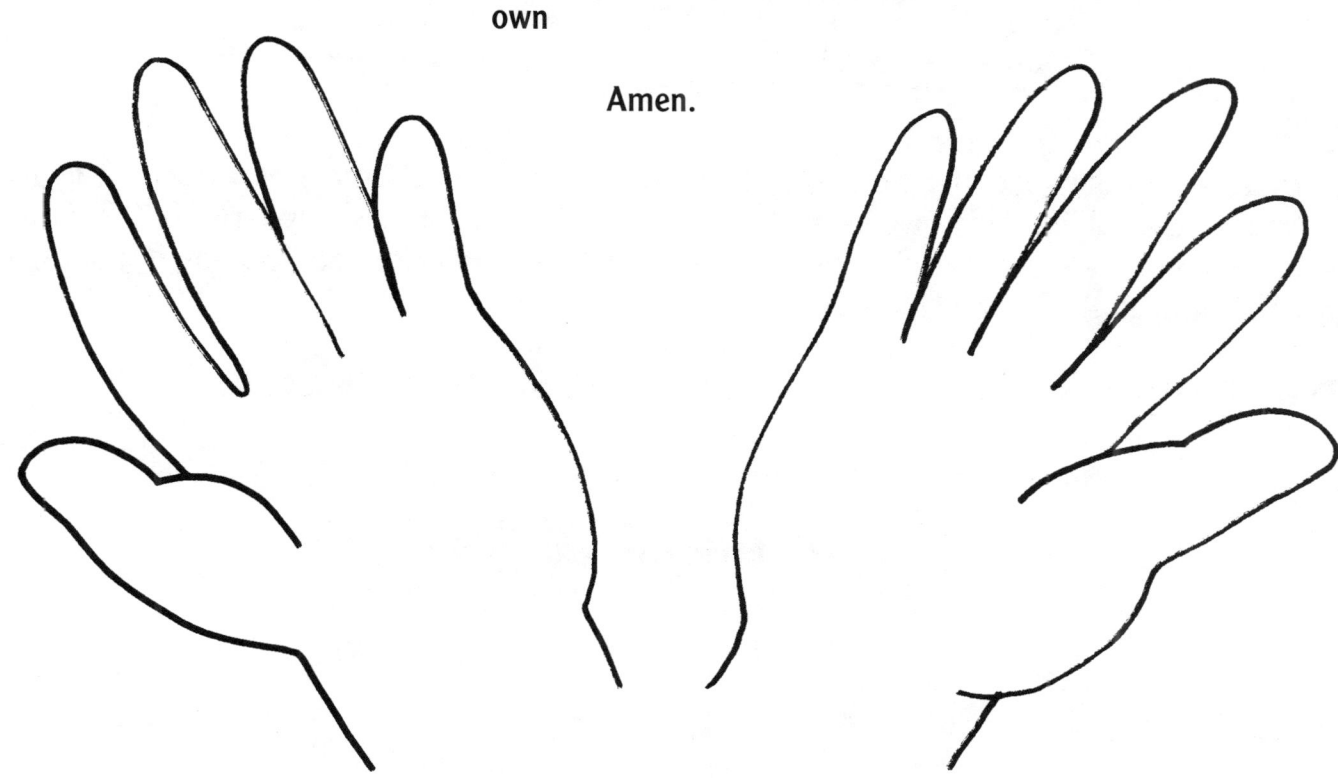

■ On the hands draw things you thank and praise God for.

Reproducible for classroom use only. Copyright © 2004 E.T. Nedder Publishing

Prayers to End the Rosary

After the last decade of the Rosary many people pray these two prayers:

Hail, holy Queen, Mother of mercy, our life, our sweetness, and our hope! To you we cry, poor banished children of Eve. To you we send up our sighs, mourning, and weeping in this valley of tears. Turn then, most gracious advocate, your eyes of mercy toward us, and after this our exile, show unto us the blessed fruit of your womb, Jesus. O clement, O loving, O sweet Virgin Mary. Pray for us, O holy Mother of God, that we may be made worthy of the promises of Christ.

■ Circle the crown that is different from the others.

O God, whose only-begotten Son, by his life, death, and resurrection has purchased for us the rewards of eternal life; grant, we beseech you, that meditating on these mysteries of the Most Holy Rosary of the Blessed Virgin Mary, we may imitate what they contain and obtain what they promise through the same Christ our Lord. Amen.

To end the Rosary, make the Sign of the Cross with the crucifix. Kiss the crucifix.

■ Put in the missing consonants from the list below to spell five promises of Christ:

p v P t n H n v n l c n r n d f s

1. Li__e E__e__ __as__i__g   2. __ap__i__e__s
                ★   ★

3. Hea__e__   4. __ea__e   5. U__i o__ with Go__
        ★   ★

Unscramble the letters above the stars (★) to spell how we get the promises:

_____

Our Lady of the Rosary: Fatima

On May 13, 1917, Mary appeared in Fatima, Portugal. Nine-year-old Lucy and her younger cousins, Francisco and Jacinta, were watching sheep. While building a play house out of rocks, they saw a ball of light settle on a small evergreen tree. In the light was a Lady in white who said she was from heaven. She asked the children to meet her on the 13th of the month for the next six months. She asked if they were willing to suffer to make up for sins and for sinners to return to God. She told them to pray the Rosary for world peace. The children did pray the Rosary every day but said only "Our Father" and "Hail, Mary." Now they began to pray the whole prayers.

When Lucy's parents heard of the vision, they thought she was lying. Her mother scolded her harshly. The Lady continued to appear and to tell the children to pray the Rosary. She called herself Our Lady of the Rosary. One month a government official kept the children from meeting the Lady. He threatened to boil them in oil unless they told the truth. Still, they stuck to their story. Mary promised that a miracle in October would help show that they were telling the truth.

During one visit the children had a vision of hell. Mary told them that sinners could be saved if they had devotion to the Immaculate Heart of Mary and made up for their sins. She directed the children to pray this prayer after each decade of the Rosary:

> **O my Jesus, forgive us our sins, save us from the fires of hell. Lead all souls to heaven, especially those in most need of your mercy.**

On Oct. 13 it rained, but 70,000 people gathered to watch. Lucy told them to close their umbrellas. At this last visit Mary asked to have a chapel built there. She said people should pray the Rosary every day and that the war being fought then (World War I) would end. She said that sinners should stop offending God and ask pardon. Then Mary vanished, and in the sky the children saw scenes of the mysteries of the Rosary. At the same time the crowd saw the sun become a white disc. It began to dance and shoot off colors. Suddenly it plunged to earth. People fell to their knees. The sun stopped and returned to its place. Everyone's wet clothes had dried!

As Mary had foretold, Francisco and Jacinta died soon after. Lucy, who entered the convent, was still living in 2004. Pope John Paul II was shot on May 13, 1981. He believed he survived because of Mary who first appeared on May 13. A year later the pope went to Fatima and visited Lucy. Each year millions of people go to the large shrine there.

■ Color the parts marked x to see what the Rosary and repentance bring.

Prayers for the Rosary

⭐ Sign of the Cross
In the name of the Father, and of the Son, and of the Holy Spirit. Amen.

⭐ Apostles' Creed
I believe in God, the Father almighty, creator of heaven and earth.

I believe in Jesus Christ, his only Son, our Lord. He was conceived by the power of the Holy Spirit and born of the Virgin Mary. He suffered under Pontius Pilate, was crucified, died, and was buried. He descended to the dead. On the third day he rose again. He ascended into heaven and is seated at the right hand of the Father. He will come again to judge the living and the dead.

I believe in the Holy Spirit, the holy catholic Church, the communion of saints, the forgiveness of sins, the resurrection of the body and the life everlasting. Amen.

⭐ Our Father
Our Father who art in heaven, hallowed be thy name; thy kingdom come; thy will be done on earth as it is in heaven. Give us this day our daily bread; and forgive us our trespasses as we forgive those who trespass against us. And lead us not into temptation, but deliver us from evil. Amen.

⭐ Hail Mary
Hail Mary, full of grace! The Lord is with you. Blessed are you among women, and blessed is the fruit of your womb, Jesus. Holy Mary, Mother of God, pray for us sinners now and at the hour of our death. Amen.

⭐ Doxology
Glory to the Father, and to the Son, and to the Holy Spirit. As it was in the beginning is now and will be forever. Amen.

⭐ After Each Decade
O my Jesus, forgive us our sins, save us from the fires of hell. Lead all souls to heaven, especially those in most need of your mercy.

⭐ Hail, Holy Queen
Hail, holy Queen, Mother of mercy, our life, our sweetness, and our hope! To you we cry, poor banished children of Eve. To you we send up our sighs, mourning, and weeping in this valley of tears. Turn then, most gracious advocate, your eyes of mercy toward us, and after this our exile, show unto us the blessed fruit of your womb, Jesus. O clement, O loving, O sweet Virgin Mary.

Pray for us, O holy Mother of God, that we may be made worthy of the promises of Christ.

⭐ Closing Prayer
O God, whose only-begotten Son, by his life, death, and resurrection has purchased for us the rewards of eternal life; grant, we beseech you, that meditating on these mysteries of the Most Holy Rosary of the Blessed Virgin Mary, we may imitate what they contain and obtain what they promise through the same Christ our Lord. Amen.

■ Color the star by the prayer when you know it by heart.

When to Pray the Rosary

In October 1571, a large fleet of Turks was on its way to attack Christian cities, including Rome. They had already conquered many lands, forcing the people to become Muslim. Pope Pius V quickly had a fleet formed from ships sent from Christian countries. This navy was unorganized, outnumbered, and sure to be defeated. The pope, however, also asked people all over Europe to pray the Rosary in public. The two navies fought in the Gulf of Lepanto — part of the Ionian Sea near Greece. Against all odds, the Christians were victorious. In memory of this event, the next pope made October 7 the feast of Our Lady of the Rosary.

When you have a special need, turn to Mary by praying the Rosary!

Rosary Facts

- October is the month of the Rosary.
- Padre Pio, who was declared a saint in 2002, called the Rosary "that weapon."
- Pope John XXIII and other holy people prayed the Rosary every day.
- People pray the Rosary when they can't fall asleep.
- Father Patrick Peyton promoted the praying of the family Rosary.
- Praying the Rosary before the Blessed Sacrament gains the forgiveness of all punishment due to sin.

■ Begin with T and on the line below write every other letter to read Father Peyton's famous motto.

■ Check when you will pray the Rosary, at least one decade.

- [ ] Before going to bed
- [ ] With my family
- [ ] To pray for peace
- [ ] When I need help
- [ ] When I am sick
- [ ] When I can't sleep
- [ ] On Saturdays, Mary's day
- [ ] Today

The Mysteries of the Rosary

During each decade of the Rosary we think about a mystery in the life of Jesus and Mary. There used to be three sets of mysteries. The first set covered events in the early life of Jesus. The second were events of his suffering and death. The third dealt with events after Jesus rose. There were no mysteries about Jesus' public life before his death. Then in 2002 Pope John Paul II gave us a new set of mysteries that filled this gap.

■ Use the code to write the names of the sets of mysteries.

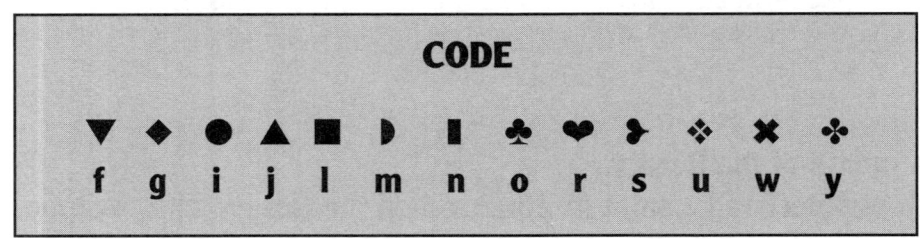

_____ Mysteries
▲ ♣ ❖ ▼ ✧ ■

2. The Annunciation
3. The Visitation
4. The Nativity
5. The Presentation in the Temple
6. The Finding of Jesus in the Temple

_____ Mysteries
◆ ■ ♣ ♥ ● ♣ ❖ ♠

1. The Resurrection
2. The Ascension
3. The Coming of the Holy Spirit
4. The Assumption of Mary
5. The Crowning of Mary

_____ Mysteries
■ ❖ ◗ ● ∎ ♣ ❖ ♠

(Mysteries of Light)
1. The Baptism of Jesus
2. Miiracle at the Wedding in Cana
3. Proclamation of the Good News
4. The Transfiguration
5. The Institution of the Eucharist

_____ Mysteries
♠ ♣ ♥ ♥ ♣ ✖ ▼ ❖ ■

1. The Agony in the Garden
2. The Scourging at the Pillar
3. The Crowning with Thorns
4. The Carrying of the Cross
5. The Crucifixion and Death of Jesus

Write the set of mysteries prayed each day of the week.

Sunday _____

Monday _____

Tuesday _____

Wednesday _____

Thursday _____

Friday _____

Saturday _____

First Joyful Mystery: The Annunciation

God sends the Angel Gabriel to Mary in the town of Nazareth. The angel tells Mary that she will have a son who will be the Son of God. He will be a king in King David's royal line. Mary is to name her son Jesus. Because Mary is not yet married to Joseph, she asks how this can be. Gabriel tells her that it will happen through the power of the Holy Spirit. He also tells Mary that her relative Elizabeth, who is old, will also have a baby. Mary answers, "Behold, I am the handmaid of the Lord. May it be done to me according to your word." (Lk 1:38)

■ Find and circle the key words in the puzzle. Some are diagonal.

Key Words

- angel
- Mary
- Joseph
- Gabriel
- Son of God
- Nazareth
- Jesus
- king
- handmaid
- Holy Spirit
- Elizabeth
- David

```
B E C I F O J E S U S
H O L Y S P I R I T A
A C D I L U N P O R N
N O N A Z A R E T H G
D I R K D A N U C L E
M E L I G A B R I E L
A A V N V H T E R B C
I A R G O S O R T N E
D R O Y J O S E P H O
S O N O F G O D I L X
```

■ Color the checked pieces to see what Mary said that changed the world.

Jesus, may I always be ready to do God's will as Mary did!

Second Joyful Mystery: The Visitation ☺

After Mary conceived Jesus, she traveled to her relative Elizabeth to help her during her pregnancy. When Elizabeth saw Mary, the baby within her, John the Baptist, jumped. Elizabeth greeted Mary as the Mother of God. Mary prayed a song praising God for his goodness to her, to the poor, and to her people, Israel.

■ Take Mary to Elizabeth through the maze.

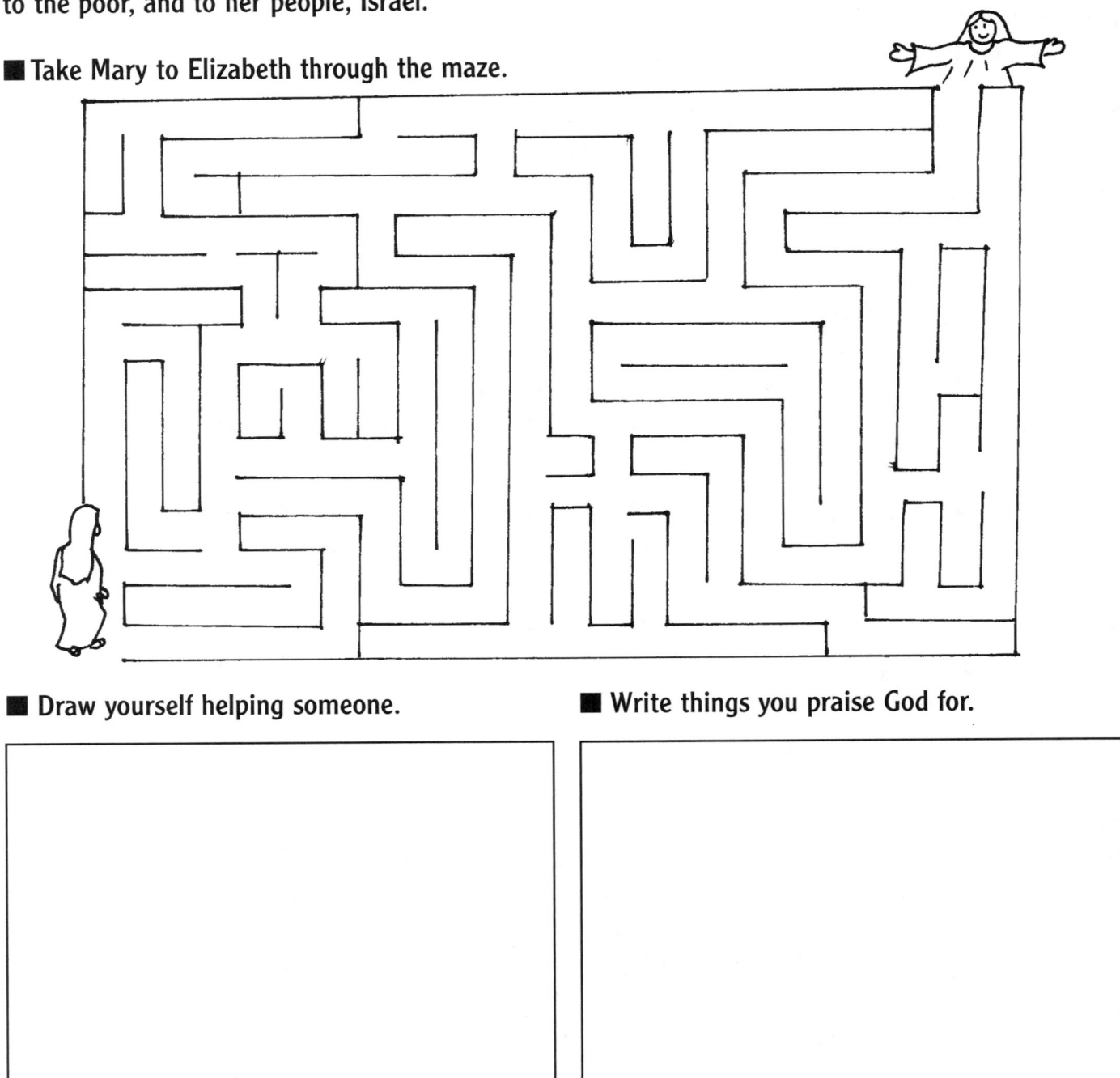

■ Draw yourself helping someone.

■ Write things you praise God for.

Jesus, may I be quick to help others!

14

Third Joyful Mystery: The Nativity 😊

Caesar Augustus decrees that all go to their hometown to be registered for a census. Mary and Joseph go to Bethlehem, city of David. Because there was no room in the inns, they stay in a stable. That night Jesus is born. Mary lays him in a manger. Angels appear to shepherds to tell the good news. Later, led by a star, wise men from the East come with gifts.

■ Connect the dots to finish the picture.

■ Unscramble the words about Jesus' birth.

nin _____   espJho _____

ryaM _____   sart _____

siwe nem _____   emhBehtle _____

pdeehhssr _____   gslnae _____

eagrmn _____   yogrl _____

Jesus, let me spread the Good News of your love!

Reproducible for classroom use only. Copyright © 2004 E.T. Nedder Publishing

Fourth Joyful Mystery: The Presentation ☺

Mary and Joseph take Jesus to the Temple to offer him to God, as all Jewish parents did with their sons. Simeon, a good man, recognizes that Jesus is the Savior. He praises God for sending Jesus, our Light. Anna, an elderly prophet who prayed in the Temple, also recognizes the Savior. Simeon tells Mary that she will suffer. We call Mary the Sorrowful Mother because of the pain she felt when Jesus was in trouble, rejected, and killed on the cross.

■ Trace the chi-rho, a symbol for Jesus, in the candle. Draw a flame on the candle and think of your baptism when your parents brought you to church and you became a child of God.

■ Write the opposites of the words below and you will see what Jesus, the light of the world, brought us.

dark _____

night _____

death _____

sadness _____

evil _____

end _____

hell _____

■ Write the letter that comes before the given one to learn what Simeon compared her pain to. Then draw one in the box.

T   X   P   S   E

Jesus, I want to walk in your light all my life!

Fifth Joyful Mystery: The Finding of Jesus in the Temple

When Jesus was 12 years old, he went to Jerusalem with Mary and Joseph for the feast of Passover. On the way home his parents missed him. They returned to Jerusalem, and three days later they found him in the Temple. He was talking to the teachers and amazing them with his knowledge. Jesus asked Mary, "Did you not know that I must be in my Father's house?" (Lk 2:49)

■ The church is our Father's house where we learn about God. Color the churches that show something that teaches us about our faith.

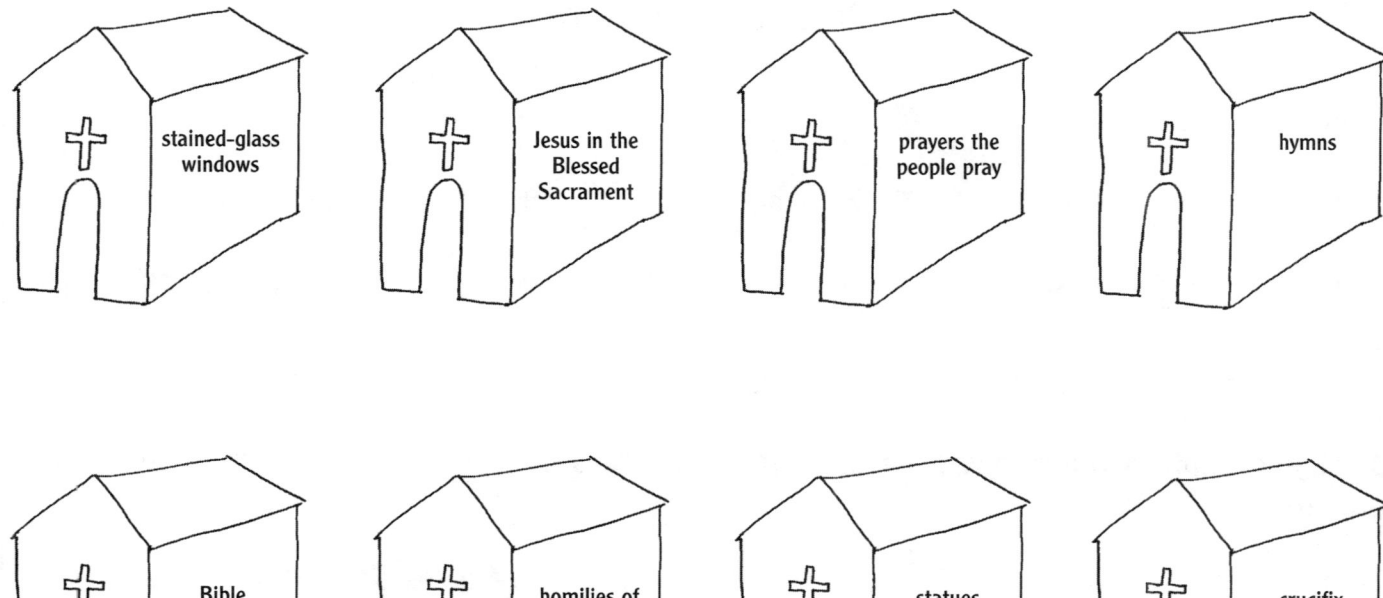

■ On the clock draw the time you go to church. Write the name of your church on the line.

Jesus, help me obey my heavenly Father by obeying my parents.

First Luminous Mystery: The Baptism of Jesus

Jesus goes to the Jordan River where John the Baptist is baptizing sinners. Baptism is a sign that they want to give up their sinful ways. Jesus asks John to baptize him. When John does, the Holy Spirit comes down on Jesus like a dove. The Father's voice is heard saying, "You are my beloved Son; with you I am well pleased." (Lk 3:22) At his baptism Jesus accepts his mission to be the Messiah.

■ Add the vowels in the words that tell what Jesus was called to be.

Mission of Jesus

- T __ __ ch __ r
- H __ __ l __ r
- S __ v __ __ r
- Pr __ ph __ t
- K __ ng
- Pr __ __ st
- S __ ff __ r __ ng S __ rv __ nt
- H __ __ d of the Ch __ rch

■ At your baptism you received a mission too. What does God call you to be? List your roles in the box.

My Mission

_____

_____

_____

_____

■ God calls every baptized person to one and the same thing. To see what it is, add the vertical lines to these letters by connecting the dots.

Heavenly Father, may I always live as your beloved child!

18

Second Luminous Mystery: Miracle at the Wedding in Cana

Mary, Jesus, and his disciples are at a wedding in Cana. The wine runs out. Mary says to Jesus, "They have no wine." He replies, "How does [this] affect me? My hour has not yet come." But Mary tells the servers, "Do whatever he tells you." Jesus has the servers fill the six large water jars with water and take some to the headwaiter. This man told the groom, "You have kept the good wine until now." (based on John 2:1-11)

■ Each jar held about 25 gallons. How many gallons of wine did Jesus make?

_____ (A vast amount!)

■ Work the crossword puzzle.

Across
2. Mary's advice: "Do ___ he tells you."
5. Jesus' followers who saw the miracle
7. Quality of wine Jesus provided
9. It became wine

Down
1. Town of Jesus' first miracle
2. Kind of party Jesus was at
3. He has power over nature
4. An unexplainable event that breaks nature's laws
6. Number of water jars
8. Person who got Jesus to help

■ How many words can you make out of the letters in *miracle* ?

_____ _____ _____ _____ _____

_____ _____ _____ _____ _____

_____ _____ _____ _____ _____

_____ _____ _____ _____ _____

Mary, help me to do whatever Jesus tells me!

Reproducible for classroom use only. Copyright © 2004 E.T. Nedder Publishing

Third Luminous Mystery: Proclamation of the Good News

Jesus proclaims the Good News that God loves us and saves us from sin and death. He tells us that God's kingdom of peace, justice, and love is near. Someday we can be with him forever.

■ Piece together some good news Jesus gave us. Break the letters in places to form messages that make sense. Write the messages on the lines.

❶

Icam esot hat t he ymig hth ave lif ea ndh aveitm oreab und ant ly.

_____

_____

John 10:10

❷

Wha tev ery ouas kt heFat herinm ynam ehew illg ivey ou.

_____

John 16:23

❸

Tak eco ura ge, I ha veco nqu ere dth ewo rld.

_____

John 16:33

❹

Bles seda ret hec lea nof he ar t fo rth eyw ills eeG od.

_____

Matthew 5:8

■ Add your artwork around Jesus' words to decorate them:

The kingdom of God is at hand. Repent, and believe in the gospel.
Mark 1:15

■ Who can you tell the Good News to? _____

Father, may your kingdom come!

Fourth Luminous Mystery: The Transfiguration

Jesus takes Peter, James, and John up a mountain. There he is transfigured. His face shines, and his clothes become dazzling white. The prophets Elijah and Moses appear and talk to Jesus about his coming suffering and death. Peter offers to make three tents for them. Then a cloud comes and a voice says, "This is my beloved Son. Listen to him." The apostles are terrified. Suddenly only Jesus is there with them. (Mk 9:7)

■ Climb the mountain by circling the first "J" and every third letter. Print these letters on the lines to show the seven persons at the Transfiguration.

1. __ __ __ __ __   3. __ __ __ __ __   5. __ __ __ __ __ __

2. __ __ __ __ __   4. __ __ __ __   6. __ __ __ __ __

                     7. __ __ __ __ __ __

■ Rearrange the letters in *listen* to spell what we must be to hear Jesus speak.

L   I   S   T   E   N   __ __ __ __ __ __

■ Write one thing Jesus tells you to do: _____

Jesus, strengthen me during hard times in my life!

Fifth Luminous Mystery: The Institution of the Eucharist

At the Last Supper with his apostles before he died, Jesus took bread, blessed and broke it and gave it to them. He said, "This is my body." Then he took a cup of wine and said, "This is my blood, which will be shed for many." Jesus ordered, "Do this in memory of me."

■ Color the pieces: y=yellow g=green b=brown p=purple x=blue r=red
Trace the letters at the bottom.

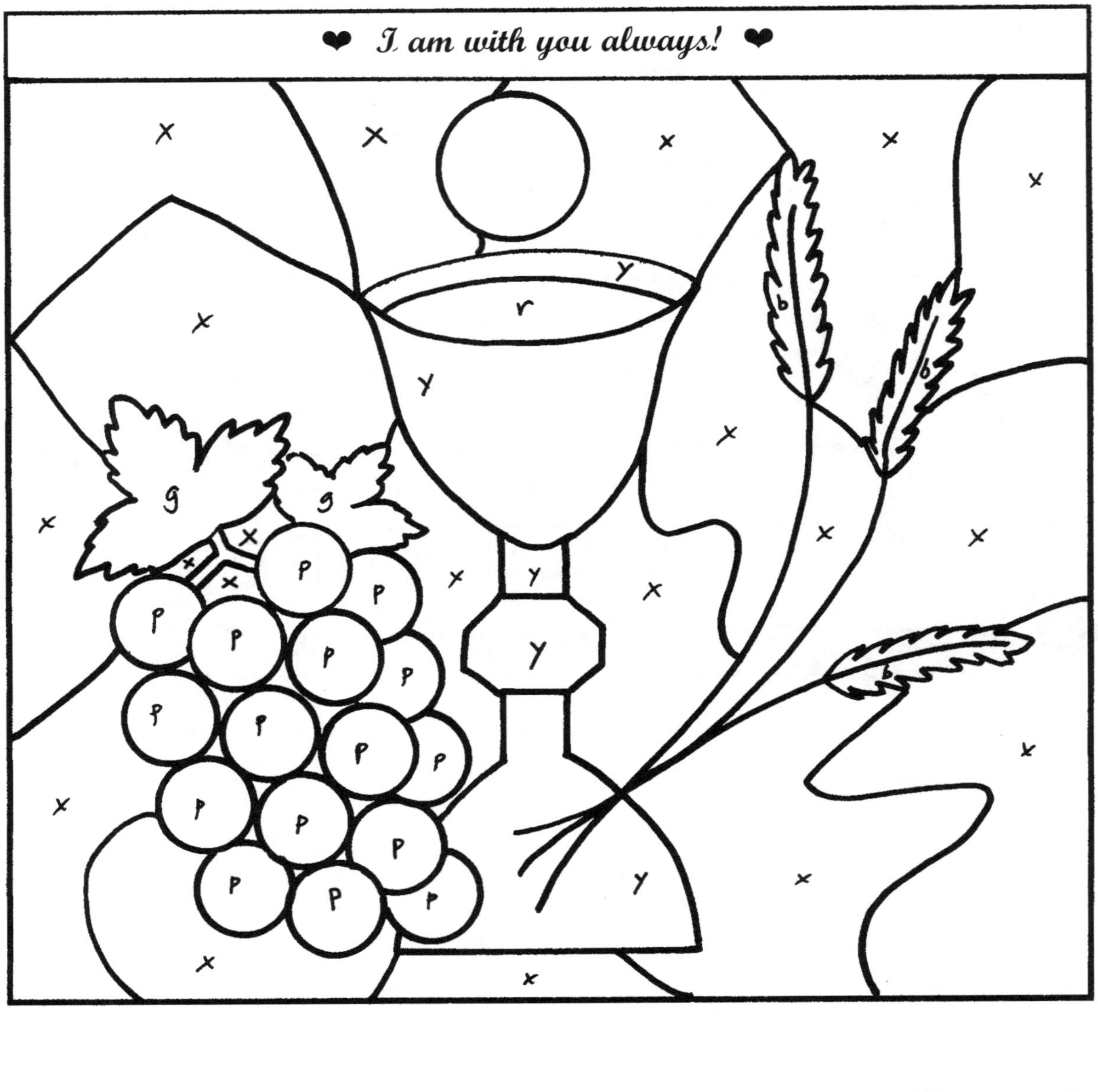

❤ *I am with you always!* ❤

My Lord and my God!

Jesus, thank you for the gift of yourself in the Eucharist!

First Sorrowful Mystery: The Agony in the Garden ☹

After the Last Supper Jesus took Peter, James, and John to a garden on the Mount of Olives. Overcome with sadness, he told them to watch and pray. Then he went a short distance away. He prayed: "My Father, if it is possible, let this cup pass from me; yet, not as I will, but as you will." (Mt 26:39). When he returned, he found the apostles asleep. He asked, "So you could not keep watch with me for one hour?" (Mt 26: 40). This happened two more times. Then soldiers came and arrested Jesus.

■ Find twelve cups hidden in the garden and circle them.

■ When will you spend some time with Jesus? _____

Father, not my will but yours be done!

Second Sorrowful Mystery: The Scourging at the Pillar ☹

Pilate found Jesus not guilty of anything, but he ordered the Roman soldiers to lash him with whips.

■ Jesus suffered for love of us. Write in the hearts something difficult you will do for love of him for each day of the coming week. Some ideas are in the pillar.

Pray a prayer for someone you don't like.

Give in to someone.

Share something.

Do not watch TV or use the computer.

Smile a lot.

Do a job very well, like your homework.

Compliment two people.

Help someone.

Clean something.

Do a secret act of love.

Give up dessert, candy, or a snack.

Visit a lonely person.

■ Color the heart when you do the act of love.

Jesus, I love you!

Third Sorrowful Mystery: The Crowning with Thorns

The soldiers wove a crown out of thorns and placed it on Jesus' head. They put a scarlet robe on him and put a reed in his hand. Then they knelt before him and mocked him as a king.

■ Unscramble the words in the crown that tell what Jesus is king of.

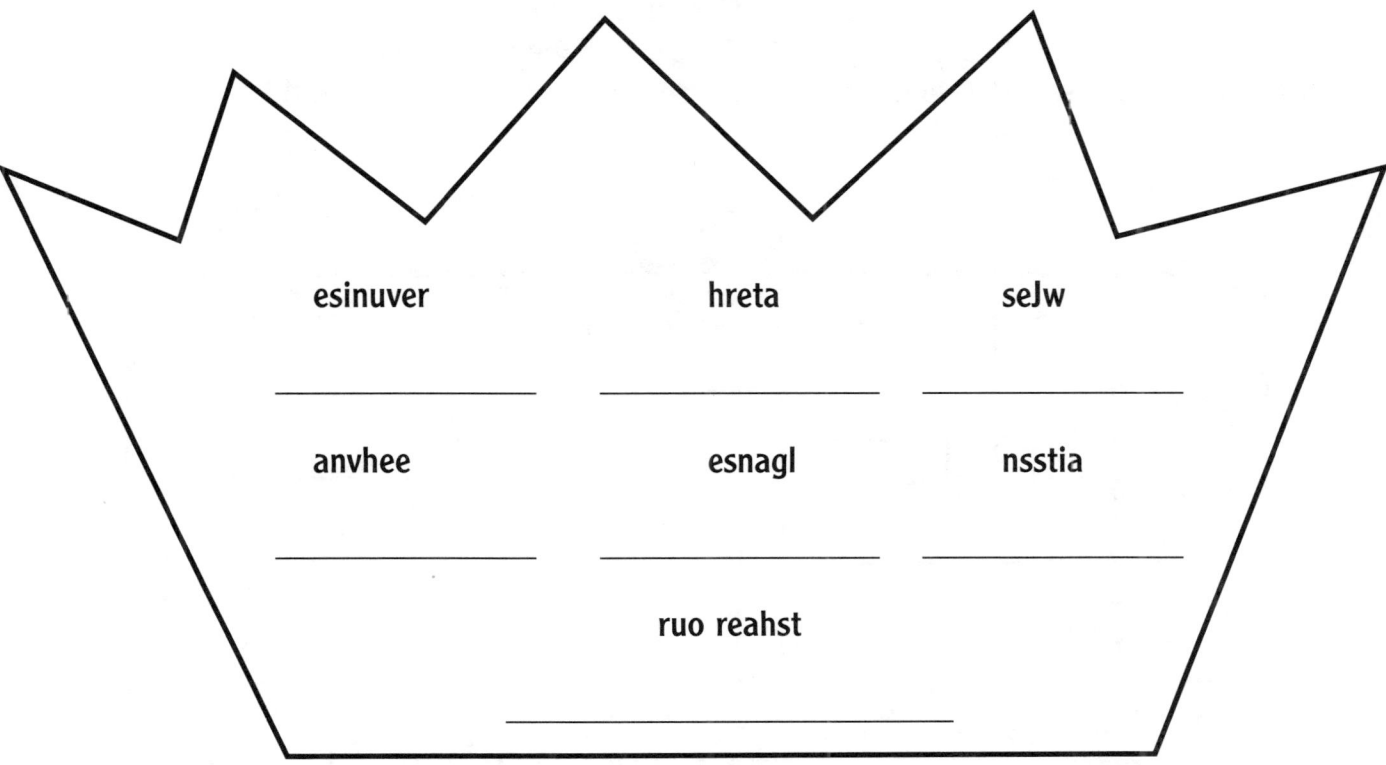

■ Cross out the letters X, Y, and Z and you will see a title of Jesus found in the last book in the Bible. (Revelation 19:16) Write it on the lines.

XY KY I XY Z NXX GY O ZF XKY XI ZY NY GXS ZXA ZNY D

__ __ __ __ __   __ __   __ __ __ __ __

Z X X L YZ O XYY R ZZ D OY F XL ZY X O ZXY R XZY D XS Y X

__ __ __ __   __ __   __ __ __ __ __

■ What feast do we celebrate on the last Sunday of the church year, the Sunday before Advent? Fill in the missing consonants.

C __ __ I __ T __ __ E __ I __ __

Jesus, may you always reign in my heart!

Fourth Sorrowful Mystery: The Carrying of the Cross

Jesus carries his cross through the streets of Jerusalem to Golgotha, the Place of the Skull, which we call Calvary. Soldiers make Simon help him.

■ Follow a path to Calvary past the stations of the cross that deal with the carrying of the cross. As you come to each station pray,
"We adore you, O Christ, and we praise you
because by your holy cross you have redeemed the world."

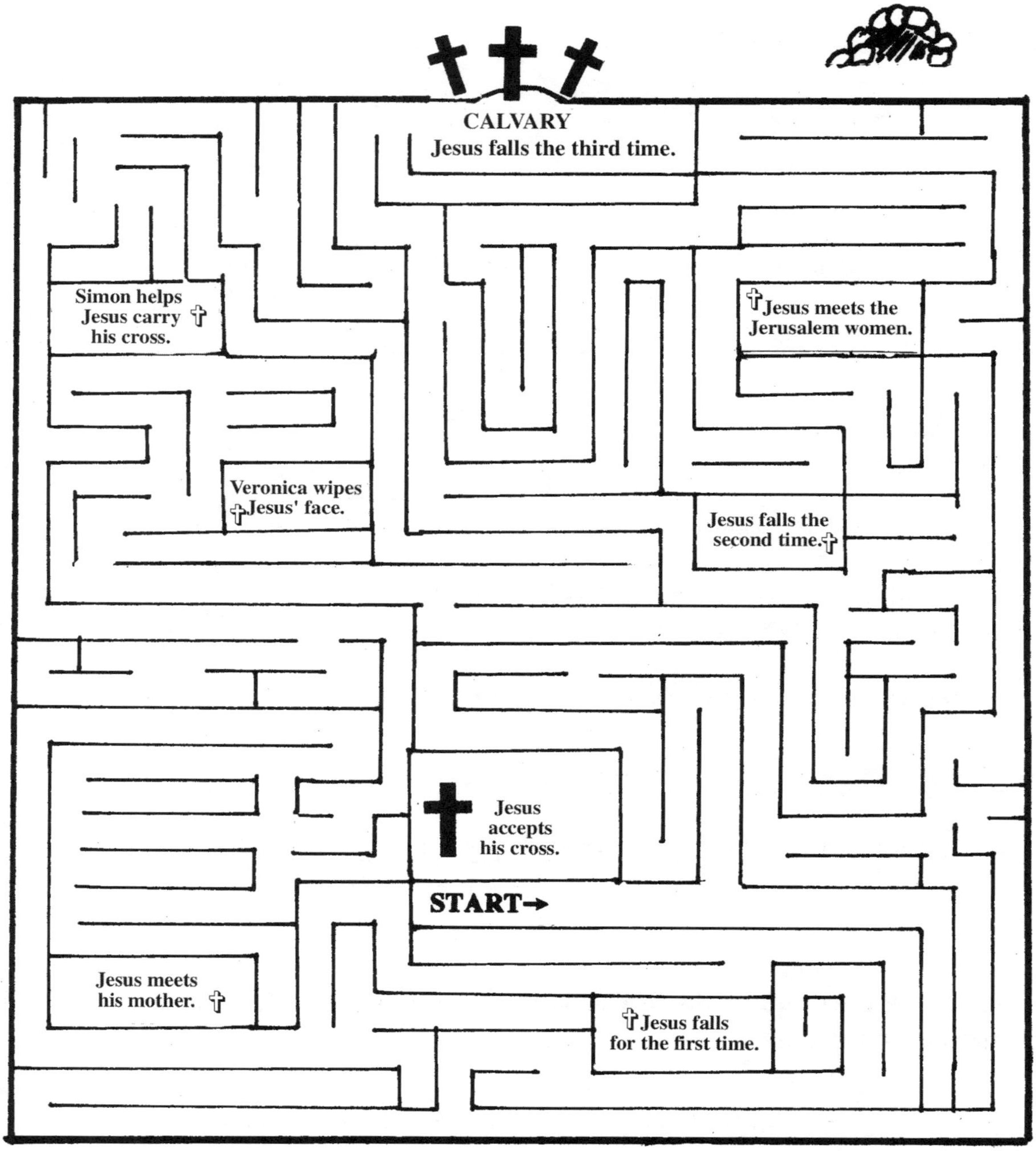

My Jesus, mercy!

Fifth Sorrowful Mystery: The Crucifixion and Death of Jesus

At noon Roman soldiers crucified Jesus between two thieves. Jesus promised the thief who didn't mock him that he would be in Paradise with him that day. Jesus said to Mary, "Woman, behold, your son," (Jn 19:26) and to John, "Behold, your mother." (Jn 19:27) The soldiers divided his clothing. About three in the afternoon Jesus said, "I thirst." (Jn 19:28) After taking some wine from a sponge, he said, "Father, into your hands I commend my spirit. It is finished," and he died. (Lk 23:46; Jn 19:30)

■ The cross is the sign of God's love for us. Write the letter of each cross by its description. In the box design your own.

____ 1. St. Andrew Cross is x-shaped as the one St. Andrew was martyred on.

____ 2. The Celtic Cross has a circle for eternity or Christians around the cross.

____ 3. The Maltese Cross from Spain has eight points for the Beatitudes.

____ 4. The Ankh (life) Cross from Egypt has a circle on top to represent life.

____ 5. The Budded Cross has three knobs at each end for the Trinity.

____ 6. The Hope Cross is an anchor, symbol of hope, which the cross gave us.

____ 7. The Tau (or St. Anthony's Cross) is in the shape of a "t".

____ 8. The Greek Cross, used by the Red Cross, is like a plus sign.

____ 9. The Jerusalem Cross is four Tau Crosses and four Greek Crosses.

____ 10. St. Peter's Cross is upside down the way Peter was crucified.

■ Write the words where they belong:

| life ◆ world ◆ Son ◆ loved ◆ everyone ◆ perish ◆ believes |

"God so _____ the _____ that he gave his only _____,

so that _____ who _____ in him might not

_____ but might have eternal _____." John 3:16

Hail, holy cross!

Reproducible for classroom use only. Copyright © 2004 E.T. Nedder Publishing

First Glorious Mystery: The Resurrection

On the third day after Jesus' death women come to his tomb with spices for his burial. They find the stone rolled away. A bright angel directs them to go tell the disciples that Jesus lives. Jesus appears to Mary Magdalene, to other women, and to two disciples on the way to Emmaus. That night he visits the apostles.

■ Put an X on the Easter symbol that is different in each row.

A chick comes out of an egg like Jesus breaks forth from his tomb with new life.

Rabbits multiply rapidly. They are a sign of the abundant new life Jesus brings.

The lamb was sacrificed to save the Jewish people at Passover. Jesus is the lamb of God who saved us by his blood and rose victorious.

A caterpillar in a cocoon comes forth as a lovely butterfly. In the same way Jesus comes forth with the new, glorified life we will have someday.

Risen Savior, I place my hope in you!

Second Glorious Mystery: The Ascension

Forty days after Jesus rose, he blessed the apostles and sent them to preach the Gospel to the ends of the earth. Then he was taken up to heaven. Two men in white told the apostles that at the end of time Jesus would return the same way.

■ Complete the mission Jesus gave his apostles in Matthew 28:19–20.

CODE

A	B	C	D	E	F	G	H	I	L	M	N	O	P	R	S	T	V	W	Y	Z
▼	✷	▢	♥	✚	◗	↔	■	♣	✤	❄	↬	○	⇨	♪	●	❩	♠	✖	⤴	▪

"__ __ , therefore, and make __ __ __ __ __ __ __ __ __ of
 G O   D I S C I P L E S

all __ __ __ __ __ __ __ , __ __ __ __ __ __ __ __
     N A T I O N S   B A P T I Z I N G

them, in the __ __ __ __ of the __ __ __ __ __ __,
              N A M E   F A T H E R

and of the Son, and of the __ __ __ __ __ __ __ __ __,
                             H O L Y   S P I R I T

__ __ __ __ __ __ __ __ them to __ __ __ __ __ __ __ all that
 T E A C H I N G   O B S E R V E

I have commanded you. And behold, I am with you __ __ __ __ __ __."
                                                  A L W A Y S

■ In the cloud draw something that Jesus commanded us to do.

Jesus, bless the work of missionaries all over the world!

Third Glorious Mystery: The Coming of the Holy Spirit

Mary and the apostles are praying in Jerusalem as Jesus said to do. On the ninth day after the ascension, the house is filled with the sound of a great wind. Tongues of fire come to rest over each person's head. Filled with the Holy Spirit, the apostles go out and courageously preach about Jesus. People who speak different languages all understand them. Three thousand people are baptized.

■ Circle the words about Pentecost in the word search.

Key Words
- nine
- Pentecost
- wind
- fire
- Mary
- apostles
- tongues
- preach
- baptize
- Holy Spirit
- Jesus
- Jerusalem

```
C B A P T I Z E W O T
M E J L R F L N U D O
A P E N T E C O S T N
R A R C I B A P Q U G
Y D U W I N D C S E U
J E S U S F E R H L E
G R A P O S T L E S S
H O L Y S P I R I T H
V R E P C L I M U J S
L I M A R F B K N U T
```

■ Unscramble the words in the flames to see some of the gifts and fruits that the Holy Spirit brings us at baptism and confirmation.

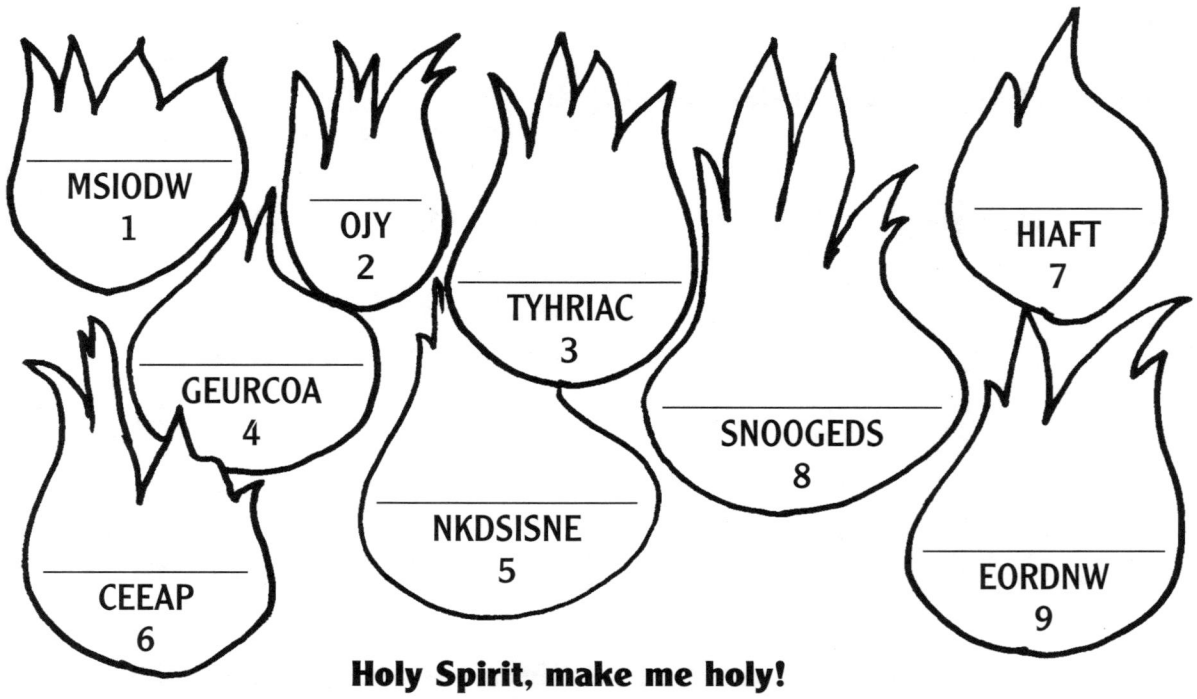

1. MSIODW
2. OJY
3. TYHRIAC
4. GEURCOA
5. NKDSISNE
6. CEEAP
7. HIAFT
8. SNOOGEDS
9. EORDNW

Holy Spirit, make me holy!

Fourth Glorious Mystery: The Assumption of Mary

At the end of her life, Mary was taken to heaven body and soul. She did not have to wait until the end of the world for her body and soul to be reunited. Mary is a sign of how we shall all be one day.

■ The prayer "The Litany of the Blessed Virgin" contains many beautiful titles for her. Check the three you like best. Put a star by your favorite.

Mother most pure	House of gold
Mother of our Redeemer	Gate of heaven
Virgin most powerful	Morning star
Virgin most faithful	Refuge of sinners
Mirror of justice	Comforter of the afflicted
Seat of wisdom	Help of Christians
Cause of our joy	Queen of martyrs
Mystical rose	Queen conceived without original sin
Tower of David	Queen of peace

■ In the boxes draw a picture of two of the titles. Write the titles on the lines.

■ Circle every third letter, beginning with "H," to see Mary's greatest title. Write it on the line.

A C H R I O Z S L U N Y R A M I W O E S T O X H C I E L A R

V B O W Y F N O G Y S O L E D _____

Mary, pray for us!

Fifth Glorious Mystery: The Crowning of Mary

Mary, the Mother of God, is queen over heaven and earth. She is our heavenly mother who intercedes for us.

The Story of Lourdes

Bernadette Soubirous was from a poor family in France. On Feb. 11, 1858, she, her sister, and a friend went to collect firewood. Bernadette had asthma so she lagged behind. At a stream, when she stopped to remove her shoes and socks, she heard a sound like wind. In a grotto she saw light around a girl dressed in white with a blue sash. A white Rosary hung on the girl's arm. Smiling, she made the Sign of the Cross with it. After Bernadette prayed the Rosary, the young lady smiled and was gone.

Three days later Bernadette returned to the grotto. During the Rosary, she saw the lady and went into a trance. Despite her parents and teachers scolding, Bernadette visited the grotto again. Now the lady asked her to come for fifteen days and said, "I don't promise to make you happy in this world but in the next."

The lady appeared these days but usually didn't speak. Police questioned Bernadette. On Feb. 24 the lady said, "Pray to God for the conversion of sinners," and had Bernadette kiss the ground for penance. The next day the lady had Bernadette dig in the dirt. A day later, water was trickling from that spot.

On March 1 among the many people at the grotto was a pregnant mother who had two paralyzed fingers. When this woman put her hand in the spring gushing from the ground, her fingers were healed!

On the following day the lady told Bernadette, "Go and tell the priests that people must come here in procession and that a chapel must be built here." When Bernadette talked to a priest, he was upset. He told her to ask the lady her name. On the feast of the Annunciation the lady appeared again and told Bernadette, "I am the Immaculate Conception." Bernadette repeated the words to the priest, not knowing what they meant. He was astounded. Only four years before, the Church had defined the doctrine of the Immaculate Conception, which means that Mary was preserved from sin from the first moment of her life.

On July 16 Bernadette saw Mary for the last time. After going to a boarding school, she entered the convent. For a time Bernadette worked in the infirmary. She died when she was only 29 and soon after, was declared a saint. Each day thousands visit the shrine of Lourdes. The Church has officially recognized 67 miracles there.

■ Write Mary, your heavenly mother, a note asking her to pray for something.

Dear Mary, _____

_____

_____

O Mary, conceived without sin, pray for us!

The Visitation	The Annunciation	
The Finding of Jesus in the Temple	The Presentation in the Temple	The Nativity
Miracle at the Wedding in Cana	The Baptism of Jesus	
The Institution of the Eucharist	The Transfiguration	Proclamation of the Good News

The Sorrowful Mysteries

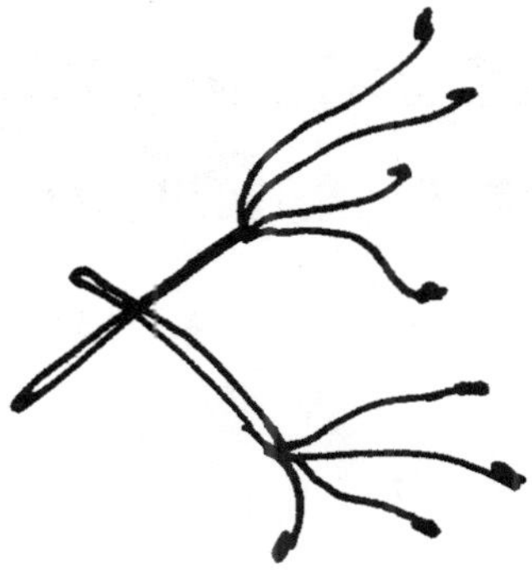

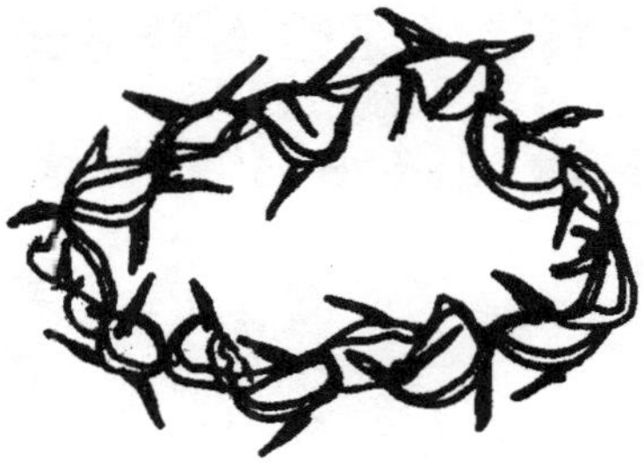

The Glorious Mysteries

The Scourging at the Pillar	**The Agony in the Garden**	
The Crucifixion and Death	**The Carrying of the Cross**	**The Crowning with Thorns**
The Ascension	**The Resurrection**	
The Crowning of Mary	**The Assumption of Mary**	**The Coming of the Holy Spirit**

Answer Key

p. 1 The Rosary
"To Mary because" she is God's mother, she is our mother, we wish to honor her, thank her, or ask a favor.

Mysteries, Decades

p. 2 Rosary Acrostic

```
        M A R Y
          R O S E
    B E A D S
        D E C A D E S
  M Y S T E R I E S
        P R A Y E R
```

Rosary Arithmetic
1. Answers will vary.
2. 15
3. 50
4. Dominic, Dominicans

p. 5 The Our Father
1. B 2. E 3. F 4. H
5. G 6. A 7. D 8. C

p. 6 The Hail Mary

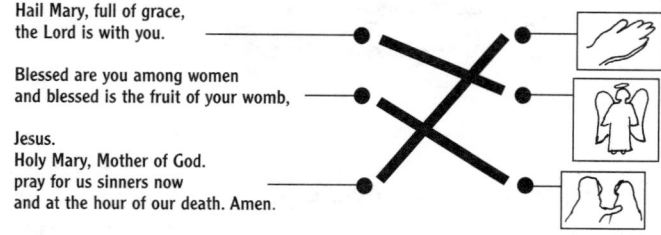

God's Wish List
All should be checked except: stay up late, take things if you won't get caught, bully others, and take dangerous dares.

p. 7 The Doxology
Father, Son, Holy Spirit, now

p. 8 Prayers to End the Rosary
The second crown in the first row is different.
1. life everlasting 2. happiness 3. heaven 4. peace

5. union with God
Scrambled word: love

p. 9 Our Lady of the Rosary: Fatima
The word is "peace."

p. 11 Rosary Facts
The family that prays together stays together.

p. 12 The Mysteries of the Rosary
Joyful, Luminous, Sorrowful, Glorious
Glorious, Joyful, Sorrowful, Glorious, Luminous, Sorrowful, Joyful

p. 13 First Joyful Mystery

```
B E C I F O J E S U S
H O L Y S P I R I T A
A C D I L U N P O R N
N O N A Z A R E T H G
D I R K D A N U C L E
M E I I G A B R I E L
A A V N V H T E R B C
I R R G O S O R T N E
D D O Y J O S E P H O
S O N O F G O D I L X
```

The word in the art is "yes."

p. 14 Second Joyful Mystery

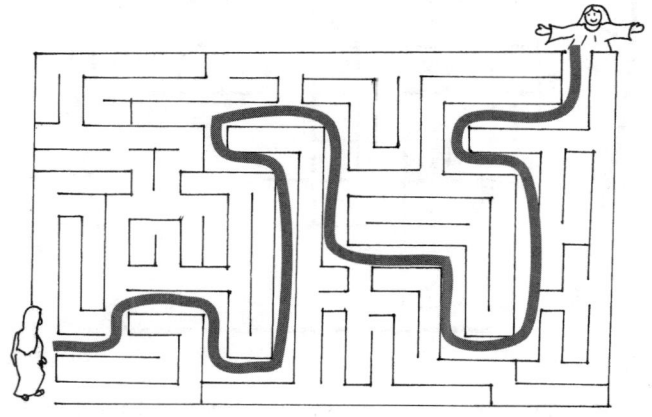

Answer Key

p. 15 Third Joyful Mystery
inn, Mary, wise men, shepherds, manger, Joseph, star, Bethlehem, angels, glory

p. 16 Fourth Joyful Mystery
Light, day, life, joy, good, beginning, heaven
Sword

p. 17 Fifth Joyful Mystery
All churches should be colored.

p. 18 First Luminous Mystery
Teacher, Prophet, Suffering servant, Healer, King, Savior, Priest, Head of the Church
My Mission (some acceptable answers): Christian, child of God, son or daughter, sister or brother, student, neighbor, player
HOLINESS

p. 19 Second Luminous Mystery
150 gallons

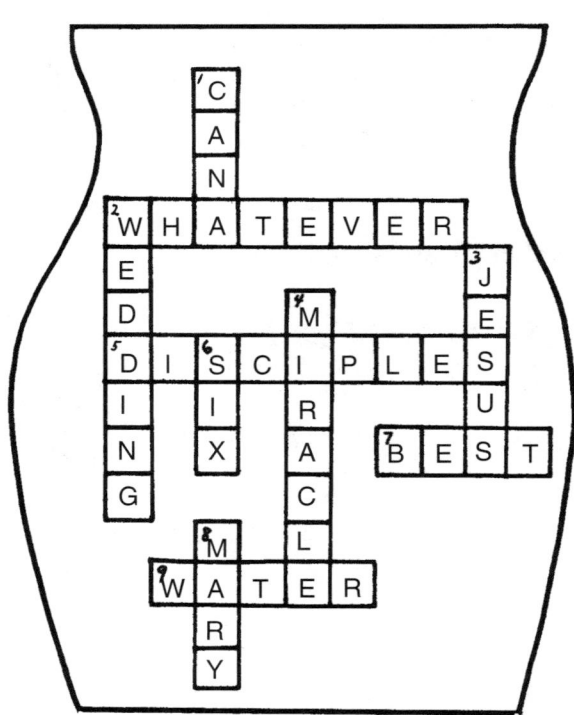

Miracle: me, ma, mace, male, mail, mailer, mar, mice, mile, ice, race, rile, real, ream, ace, aim, arm, ale, act, air, car, care, clam, clear, clime, came, camel, cram, cream, lace, liar, lair, lime, lie, ear, earl, emir

p. 20 Third Luminous Mystery
I came so that they might have life and have it more abundantly.

Whatever you ask the father in my name he will give you.

Take courage, I have conquered the world.

Blessed are the clean of heart for they will see God.

Who can you tell the Good News to? (many acceptable answers)

p. 21 Fourth Luminous Mystery
1. Jesus   2. Peter   3. James   4. John
5. Moses   6. Elijah   7. Father
Listen: silent

p. 23 First Sorrowful Mystery

p. 25 Third Sorrowful Mystery
universe, earth, Jews, heaven, angels, saints, our hearts
King of Kings and Lord of Lords
Christ the King

Answer Key

p. 26 Fourth Sorrowful Mystery

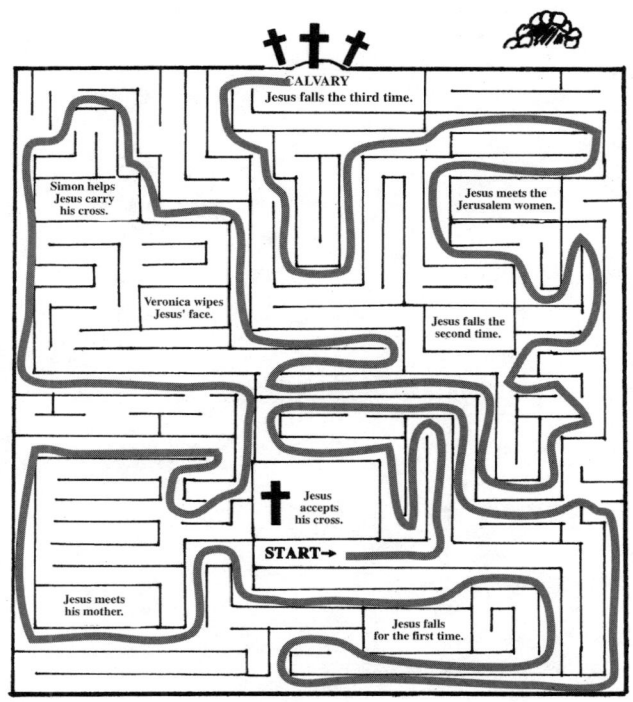

1. wisdom
2. joy
3. charity
4. courage
5. kindness
6. peace
7. faith
8. goodness
9. wonder

p. 31 Fourth Glorious Mystery
Holy Mother of God

p. 27 Fifth Sorrowful Mystery
1. C, 2. I, 3. F, 4. J, 5. B, 6. G, 7. H, 8. A, 9. D, 10. E

loved, world, So, everyone, believes, perish, life

p. 28 First Glorious Mystery
Last egg, second rabbit, first lamb, third butterfly

p. 29 Second Glorious Mystery
Go, disciples, nations, baptizing, name, Father, Holy Spirit, teaching, observe, always.

p. 30 Third Glorious Mystery

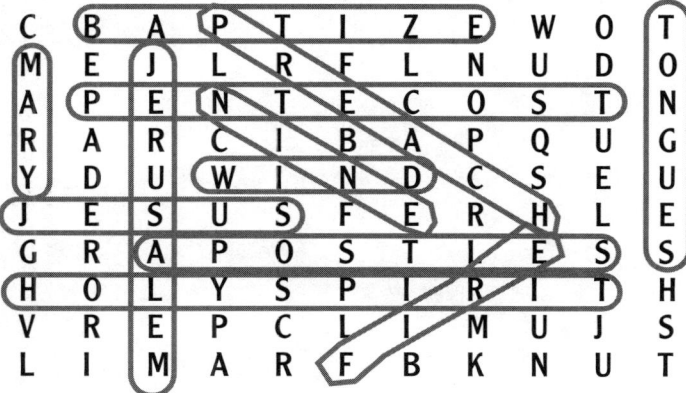

Notes